DiSCUSSiON MANUAL for STUDENT RELATiONSHiPS

TEMPTATION

DATING

SEX ?

LONELINESS ?

PARENTS ?

LOVE ?

WRiTTEN BY
DAN WEBSTER
AND
DAWSON McALLiSTER

ART BY
JiM LAMB

© Shepherd Productions, Inc., 1975
Moody Press Edition 1979

ISBN: 0 - 8024 - 2238 - 1

Printed in the United States of America

Discussion Manual for Student Relationships

The youth of America are facing problems that are seemingly insurmountable. The breakdown of the home is almost the norm for today's society. Lawlessness on the part of the young is already statistically staggering and is on the increase.

Such problems as loneliness, doubt, misuse of sex, powerful temptation, guilt, low self-esteem and other personal and relationship-oriented problems are plaguing countless thousands of people. Satan and the powers of darkness would like the student of today to think that there are no answers to the problems --except answers that man himself can invent. There could be no bigger lie.

God has clearly set down solutions to man's basic needs. He has sent Christ to pay for man's sins, and to be a light to man who is so in need of moral guidance. God has also revealed in His Word(the Bible) the basic guidelines to follow as men face the problems that life and sin bring.

God is not vague on answers to living; He speaks clearly and openly on life's issues. It is with this thought in mind that the authors conceived this manual. The authors realize that one cannot "can" answers to meet the total complexities of each person's detailed problems. However, God gives clear principles in the Bible that will work for the Christian if he will but dig them out, obey and practice them.

Dawson McAllister

Dawson McAllister is an intense, dynamic youth speaker who has a deep love for the young --for their special problems and for their spiritual growth.

Speaking in classrooms, assemblies, free speech rallies, conferences and on television, Dawson has met thousands of teenagers and young adults personally, all over the U.S., and has been impressed by the great needs in the area of relationships.

Dawson and his associate, Dan Webster, formulated this _Discussion Manual for Student Relationships_ as one way to address this evident need. This material is a reflection of hundreds of hours spent in careful research, evaluation and study by both men.

But this manual is not a theoretical construct; rather, it has the added dimension of being based on Dawson's own personal experience in dealing "one-on-one" with the very real needs of hundreds of young persons and their problems in establishing healthy relationships. This personal involvement began when Dawson was running a coffee house ministry for kids in the drug culture in Los Angeles. It has grown to an outreach that involves him in a variety of speaking, seminar, and "gut-level" evangelism situations in every part of the country.

There is no intention by Dawson McAllister to present this material as the "final answer" for kids in relationship counseling. This manual, like the popular _Discussion Manual for Student Discipleship_, is constantly being very carefully tested in actual situations and, when necessary, even in minor areas, edited and revised.

Dawson McAllister is a graduate of Bethel College (Minn.) and studied theology at Talbot Theological Seminary in Los Angeles, where he is completing his thesis on religious television programming for youth.

Dan Webster

Dan Webster draws the insights shared in this material from a knowledge of God's Word, and from his personal involvement with the special relationship problems faced by young persons he has counseled.

He has been trained in youth counselling work as a graduate of Biola College in Los Angeles. For five years he has been active in meeting the needs of hundreds of teenagers as a youth worker at Garden Grove Community Church in Garden Grove, California. It is here, in this huge suburban church, that Dan is able to see which methods are really effective in making Biblical principles real to kids on a day-by-day, year-by-year context.

Dan has also had extensive experience in youth probation work. He was, with Dawson McAllister, co-author of the _Discussion Manual for Student Discipleship_, along with this second volume.

Dan and his wife, Judy, reside in Orange, California.

Jim Lamb

As this manual was being developed (along with the _Discussion Manual for Student Discipleship_), an art character was needed that would make this material more "digestible" for a young reader. This cartoon character had to have a special, slightly humorous and very human nature that would appeal to both sexes; and his foibles, development and growth had to be an easily identifiable pattern of behavior. And this all had to be handled in such a manner so that the Biblical concepts, not the cartoons, predominated.

Jim Lamb developed this figure and was able to meet these special requirements. As a professional artist who must meet the daily challenges of the competitive commercial art field, Jim brings a unique combination of gifts into any project he undertakes.

Jim has done numerous projects for several Christian publishing companies and is polished and versatile with all the artist's mediums. His training (besides a Navy stint) has included Burnley School of Art in Seattle and Art Center College of Design in Los Angeles. He is also a graduate of Multnomah School of the Bible in Portland.

Currently, Jim is an artist/illustrator associated with Christian Brothers Visual Communication in Newport Beach, California.

HOW TO USE THIS MANUAL

●This _Discussion_ _Manual_ _for_ _Student_ _Relationships_ can be used quite effectively as a small group Bible study tool.✱

●The manual can also be used as a one-on-one sharing/discipleship tool. (Needless to say, some chapters are lengthier than others, so care should be taken to select specific parts of certain chapters for concentrated sharing of the Biblical principles here.)

●This manual can be used for your own personal Bible study--or for the personal Bible study of someone you are discipling. The manual shouldn't be given out indiscriminately, but selectively with care and concern on the part of the giver.

QUESTIONS IN THIS MATERIAL.

There were two essential purposes in the author's minds in the selection, style and placement of the questions found in this manual.

FIRST, the questions are asked to provoke users to meaningful thought and discussion. Such encounters can sometimes be more helpful to the new Christian than all the rest of his/her reading of the manual.

SECOND, the questions are obviously used in some places to bring out a point, or just to make Scripture a bit clearer in a specific application to the reader. Some of the questions may seem simplistic, and the answers are provided in parentheses under nearly every question. But the exercise of considering the thought in the question is important.

THE ART.

This manual's cartoon/illustrations were selected for visual focus on a Biblical principle, and not essentially for humor(although humor can be discovered in many of the illustrations). Make sure that the new believer takes a concentrated look at the artwork, and understands what is being visualized thoroughly.

MATERIAL PLACEMENT.

Each discussion chapter builds somewhat on the preceding material. It would be wise to follow this intended progression as the manual gets "deeper," unless a specific need can be met by directing the young believer to a specific discussion chapter.

TABLE OF CONTENTS

The Bible . . . . Page 1

God's Will . . . . Page 17

Self-Image . . . . Page 39

Loneliness . . . . Page 63

Parents . . . . Page 83

Sex . . . . Page 99

Dating . . . . Page 119

Love . . . . Page 139

Clearing The Mind . . . . Page 155

Temptation . . . . Page 169

The importance of understanding
THE BIBLE,
A COUNSELING BOOK
DiSCUSSiON 1

FRUSTRATiON...

...though not a pleasant sensation, claims countless victims --people who are acquainted with no other response to life's many puzzles. Frustration has a heyday especially among students, because the list of problems encountered by students is very lengthy.

THE LiST GOeS ON AND ON...

- *loneliness*
  - *friction in the home*
    - *misuse of sex*
      - *sense of inferiority*
        - *bitterness and rebellion*
          - *confusion concerning marriage*

- *temptation*
  - *materialism*
    - *mind pollution*
      - *hate*
        - *drugs and alcohol*
          - *disillusionment with life and general meaninglessness*

Love, joy, peace, happiness, fulfillment, the deepest desires of a person's heart are constantly assaulted and usually defeated by frustration over everyday problems. Why does life treat us this way?

1

LET'S CONSIDER FOUR QUESTIONS...

I. How did God originally intend to make people happy and fulfilled?

II. What went wrong with this plan?

III. Can what went wrong be made right again?

IV. What should be our attitude as we attempt to puzzle our way through life's frustrations?

LET'S GET INTO THE ANSWERS.

I. HOW DID GOD ORIGINALLY INTEND TO MAKE PEOPLE HAPPY AND FULFILLED?

To build a complete understanding of meaningful living, we must begin with a spiritual foundation; a foundation consisting of an understanding of God and His design for life.

Jeremiah 9:23-24

(23) *"Thus says the Lord, 'Let not a wise man boast of his wisdom, and let not the mighty man boast of his might, let not a rich man boast of*

(24) *his riches; but let him who boasts boast of this, that he understands and knows Me, that I am the Lord who exercises lovingkindness, justice, and righteousness on earth; for I delight in these things,' declares the Lord."*

According to God, life isn't a hit or miss proposition. <u>*He claims to provide trustworthy guidance to those who build upon the right spiritual foundation.*</u>

2

✱ *In verse 23, God, through the prophet Jeremiah, warns against building upon any of three specific untrustworthy foundations. What are they?*

1. wisdom
2. riches
3. mighty

FiRST, *God warns us not to trust in human wisdom. Our minds are too limited. Even if someone fed us raw knowledge until our minds became completely saturated, the mysteries of life would still surpass our ability to comprehend. Human wisdom can provide only a shaky foundation.*

SeCOND, *God warns us not to trust in our own might. Only a fool dares to consider his own personal strength and determination adequate to cope with every conceivable situation. God holds each of our lives delicately in the balance. By allowing this balance to slip just a bit, God can permit the circumstances to arise in such a way that no amount of human effort could modify their outcome.*

<u>*Think of some circumstances:*</u>

_____

_____

_____

_____

_____

THiRD, *God warns us not to trust in riches. Material blessings are no more secure than a nation's economy. Need more be said? Think of other reasons why riches could fail as the foundation of a person's life.* _____

_____

_____

God clearly wants us to understand that those who trust in their own wisdom, might, or riches build on a loose-jointed foundation. A self-made man is a weak man.

In verse 24, God provides us with a trustworthy foundation, one upon which we can build with complete confidence.

Jeremiah 9:24
"'But let him who boasts boast of this, that he understands and knows Me, that I am the Lord who exercises lovingkindness, justice, and righteousness on earth; for I delight in these things,' declares the Lord."

✳ According to verse 24, what is the key to successful living? *Exercise Lovingkindness, justice, righteousn*

✳ What does it mean to know God? _____

_____

_____

✳ According to the last part of verse 24, an understanding of God incorporates a knowledge of how He acts and moves in our lives. What are three characteristics of the way God acts?

_____

_____

THE THREE WAYS ARE...

1. _God acts in lovingkindness._ God is willing and able to show mercy, kindness, and an active love to an unworthy people.

Psalm 143:8
"Let me hear thy lovingkingness in the morning; For I trust in Thee: Teach me the way in which I should walk; For to Thee I lift up my soul."

✳ In what practical way does the Psalmist expect God to show lovingkindness? *Let me hear in the moring And That I trust in you.*

✳ What is meant by "teach me in the way I should walk?" *what why I should go, believe in him the right way.*

4

As we face life's situations, we need God's love in action, not just to comfort and encourage us, but also to show us how to walk day by day and to be more conformed to Him and His will.

2. _God acts in justice._ This is God's unique way of dealing with us in complete fairness and teaching us to respect the rights of others.

Proverbs 21:2-3
(2)"Every man's ways are right in his own eyes, But the Lord weighs the
(3)hearts. To do righteousness and justice Is desired by the Lord rather than sacrifice."

Since God deals with us justly, He counsels us to deal justly with our fellow humans, respecting their basic human rights. When we ignore His counsel, misunderstanding and heartbreak occurs between us and others. We should realize that every person has the right to privacy, understanding, respect, rights to his own property, and to be talked to and about with kindness.

Proverbs 16:7
"When a man's ways are pleasing to the Lord, He makes even his enemies to be at peace with him."

When we look at God's example of justice and follow His view of fairness in dealing with people, He will bring peace to our daily relationships and cause happiness to come into our lives. We can see how important His counsel is!

3. _God acts in righteousness._ This is God in action doing things absolutely morally right with no crookedness at all. His character is the standard for what is morally right. _And since God acts only in the right way, the counsel which God gives is absolutely right:_

Proverbs 4:18
"But the past of the righteous is like the light of dawn that shines brighter until the full day..."

Proverbs 2:7-8
(7)"He stores up sound wisdom for the upright; He is a shield to those
(8)who walk in integrity, Guarding the paths of justice, And He preserves the way of His godly ones."

✳ *If we walk in a morally upright way before God, according to this passage, what four things does God do for us?* Stores good wisdom for the upright, He's a sheild, Guards the paths of justice, preserves the way of his godly ones.

IN REVIEW THEN, WHAT IS GOD'S PLAN FOR US?

...It is that we don't trust in our wisdom, might, riches, but that we trust, know and understand Him. We understand all of this by this knowing His counsel on how to live.

IF GOD'S PLAN IS SO GREAT, WHAT IN THE WORLD HAS GONE WRONG TO MAKE MEN SO MISERABLE?

II.*THE BIG PROBLEM IS THAT MAN HAS IGNORED BOTH GOD AND HIS COUNSEL.*

Romans 3:10-11
"There is none righteous, not even one;
There is none who understands,
There is none who seeks for God:"

GOD SAYS HE IS RIGHTEOUS, AND MORALLY RIGHT. HE WANTS US TO BE RIGHTEOUS TOO.

✳ *According to the above verses from Romans, does anyone listen to God and live righteously?* no

GOD SAYS HE WANTS US TO UNDERSTAND THAT, WITH THE RIGHT ATTITUDE, WE CAN DEVELOP THE CAPACITY TO KNOW HIM.

✱ *According to the above verse, has anyone developed that ability to understand God on his own?* _yea_

GOD SAYS OUR TOP PRIORITY IS NOT WISDOM OR MIGHT OR RICHES, BUT RATHER TO SEEK AFTER HIM.

✱ *According to the verses, does anyone seek after God?* _____

We BROKE UP WITH GOD

Because God is holy and man has turned his back on God, man has broken off fellowship with God. Man has also broken off the understanding that comes from God's counsel. Now, the man who trusts in his own wisdom, might, and riches continues to make wrong decisions as he is at a loss as to which direction to go in life. "It is as though he were on a path in the jungle at night with no light to show him the way."

Proverbs 4:19
"The way of the wicked is like darkness;
They do not know over what they stumble."

III. *HOW CAN WE FIND WHAT IT TAKES TO BE HAPPY AND FULFILLED IN LIFE?*

John 8:12
"Again therefore Jesus spoke to them, saying, 'I am the light of the world; he who follows Me shall not walk in the darkness, but shall have the light of life.'"

GOD TOOK ACTION

When Christ died on the cross and rose again for man's sin, He provided a way for man to have peace with God and opened the floodgates for God to once again pour out his practical counsel for an overflowing life.

✳ According to verse 12, if we follow Jesus Christ, what will be the condition of our daily walk? _They will have the light of life_

GOD'S POWER, LOVE AND COUNSEL

God has revealed Christ to pay for man's sin and to give man the power to live a life that is pleasing to God. God had poured forth His counsel, which contains practical guidelines to living, even before Christ died. This counsel is found in the Bible. Now, as Christians, we can be assured of a growing understanding of God's loving counsel if we follow the teaching of His Word.

II Timothy 3:16
"All Scripture is inspired by God and profitable for <u>teaching</u>, for <u>reproof</u>, for <u>correction</u>, for <u>training</u> <u>in</u> <u>righteousness</u>..."

This passage clearly shows us that God is truly interested in using His Word in four areas of our lives.

1. Teaching   There are many paths in life that a person can take--some are disastrous... God and His Word teach us to take the right path.

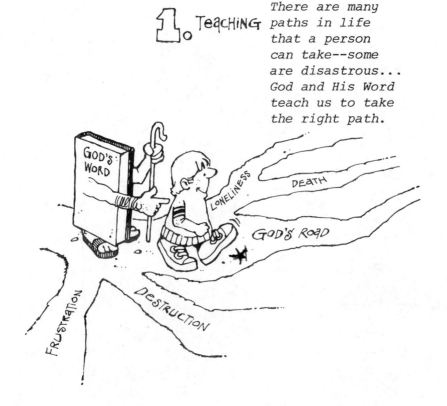

2. REPROOF

Sometimes in walking down God's path, we rebel and get off the path... The Bible tells us where we have gotten off the path.

3. CORRECTION

God corrects us through His Word and shows us how to get back on His path.

4. TRAINING

Once we get back on the path, God does not just leave us there, but gives us practical instruction on how to lead a life of peace and meaning.

Because God's Word is so great, and because it gives such real answers to life, King David could say of it:

Psalm 40:7-8
"Then I said, 'Behold, I come;
In the scroll of the book <u>it is written of me</u>;
I delight to do Thy will, O my God;
Thy Law is within my heart.'"

Psalm 19:7-10
(7)"The law of the Lord is <u>perfect</u>, restoring the soul;
    The testimony of the Lord is <u>sure</u>, making wise the simple.
(8)The precepts of the Lord are <u>right</u>, rejoicing the heart;
    The commandment of the Lord is <u>pure</u>, enlightening the eyes.
(9)The fear of the Lord is <u>clean</u>, enduring forever;
    The judgments of the Lord are <u>true</u>; they are righteous altogether.
(10)They are more desirable than gold, yes, than much fine gold;
    Sweeter also than honey and the drippings of the honeycomb."

Psalm 119:9-11
"How can a young man keep his way pure?
By keeping it according to Thy word.
(10)With all my heart I have sought Thee;
Do not let me wander from Thy commandments
(11)Thy word I have treasured in my heart,
That I may not sin against Thee."

Psalm 119:92
"If Thy law had not been my delight,
Then I would have perished in my affliction."

GET INTO THE GOOD STUFF

From the above passages, list some of the things God's Word can do for us as we discover insights in it--then <u>apply them in our lives and obey the things it says we should do.</u>

IV. *WHAT SHOULD OUR ATTITUDE BE AS WE LOOK FOR GOD'S ANSWERS TO LIVING, AS REVEALED IN THE BIBLE?*

A. We should have an attitude of <u>seeking</u>.

Proverbs 2:3-6

(3) For if you cry for discernment(this is the ability to know right from
    wrong), Lift your voice for understanding(this is the sensitivity to
(4) see life more and more as God does); If you seek her as silver, And
(5) search for her as for hidden treasures; Then you will discern the
    fear of the Lord, And discover the knowledge of God. For the Lord
(6) gives wisdom; From His mouth come knowledge and understanding. "

✱ We know that true discernment comes from God and His word. We see
  from the passage above that we are to seek God's counsel as a miner
  seeks gold. What are some of the attributes of a person who would
  look for gold? _____

  _____

Just as it would be difficult for any
gold miner to find gold without the
attitude of patience, perserverance,
diligence, determination, and in-depth
searching, so it is with the believer
who is seeking God's wisdom from His
Word. God's wisdom does not come from
a superficial reading of the Bible,
but from an intense and sincere
study of His counsel.

KEEP SEARCHIN'...

✱ Why do you think one must truly search the Scriptures in order to
  find God's guidelines for successful living? _____

  _____

(God has made His principles and loving answers available to those
who are truly searching--not just to the casual reader. If it were
otherwise, we would just use God, taking His rewards and answers, but
spending little time loving Him, and adjusting our lives to His ways
and His holiness.)

B. We must have an attitude of forsaking the sin which is prevalent
   in our lives.

James 1:21
"Therefore putting aside all filthiness and all that remains of
wickedness, in humility receive the word implanted, which is able
to save your souls."

✳ What does "putting aside" mean? _____

_____

✳ What does "filthiness" mean? _____

_____

Let's say you meet someone you are really
attracted to. You decide to go on a date
together. You probably would not show up
in your oldest, smelliest clothes to seek
to find out about that person. In a much
greater way we offend God by coming to Him
and His Word without stripping those sins
from our lives that are filthy to Him and
prevent Him from truly showing us His ways.

𝐶. We must come with <u>an attitude of humility and with a teachable
spirit</u>.

James 1:21
"Therefore putting aside all filthiness and all that remains of
wickedness, <u>in humility</u> receive the word implanted, which is able
to save your souls."

✳ What does "in humility receive the word" mean? _____

_____

Why is it harmful to come to God's Word with a rebellious

_____

IT'S YOUR ATTITUDE.

If you come to God's Word with a clenched
fist(mentally), expect to be frustrated.
He wants you to have a teachable attitude
that shows willingness to being molded
by Him and receptive to what He has
for you.

D. We must come to God's Word with an attitude that is <u>ready to act</u>
<u>in a tangible way to God's leading</u>.

James 1:22-25
(22)"But prove yourselves doers of the word, and not merely hearers who
(23)delude themselves. For if any one is a hearer of the word and not a
    doer, he is like a man who looks at his natural face in a mirror;
(24)for once he has looked at himself and gone away, he has immediately
(25)forgotten what kind of person he was. But one who looks intently at
    the perfect law, the law of liberty and abides by it, not having
    become a forgetful hearer but an effectual doer, this man shall be
    blessed in what he does."

 According to verse 22, what does a person do to himself when he hears
the Word, understands it, but doesn't act on it? _____

_____

13

THE FAKE-OUT SYNDROME

Say you get up early at 7:00 a.m. and look in the mirror. Your hair needs to be combed because it's a mess, your face needs to be washed because it's dirty, but you walk away and forget the mess you saw. Therefore, going to the mirror was a silly exercise, for it didn't help you improve the way you look. The fault was not with the mirror but with you because you did not respond to what it showed you. The Bible is a mirror. It tells us our spiritual needs and what to do about them, but if we do nothing about these areas, we show by our actions that we don't really intend to be adapt our lives to God's plan and His ways as for us. This is doubly foolish since we can never fool God about anything; break this "syndrome" by seeking God's insights in His Word, and when you find them, do them!

PROJECT:

1. Thank God for His Word and His counsel.

2. Ask God to give you the desire to seek Him and His ways.

3. Thank Him that He has provided a way of peace and happiness for you, through discovering and following His ways of life, and adapting and adjusting when He points areas for change in you.

NOTES

The importance of knowing
GOD'S WILL
Discussion 2

INTRODUCTION:
If you're a person who's committed to Christ, you probably have a desire to know God's will for your life.

You are probably asking some pressing and important questions, such as...

* Does God want me to become a professional Christian worker?

* Does God want me to get married?

* If so, who is this person, and when should we get married?

* What school does he want me to attend when I graduate?

* Does God want me to live at home after I graduate?

* Who does God want me to choose as close friends?

God's ANSWERS Are BETTER THAN ALL oTHERS!
If you are concerned about God having an influential role in answering these questions, then you're right where you should be. God greatly desires for you to seek His counsel and His will in every area of life.

> To begin with, the key to life is to seek, know and follow God's will for you as He reveals this will to you.

Jesus' whole life on earth was an example of how important it is to do God's will.

John 6:38
"For I have come down from heaven, not to do My own will, but to do the will of Him who sent Me."

John 4:34
"Jesus said to them, 'My food is to do the will of Him who sent Me, and to accomplish His work.'"

Jesus Christ, Who is God, humbled Himself and became as a man, giving us an example of how we should live. Seeking His Father's will was His primary goal. He proved how much the Father's will meant to Him when doing it would lead Him to certain shame and death.

In the Garden of Gethsemane He prayed...

Matthew 26:39
"And He went a little beyond them, and fell on His face and prayed, saying, "My Father, if it is possible, let this cup pass from Me; yet not as I will, but as Thou wilt."

✳. *If Jesus Christ spent His whole life seeking and doing the Father's will, do you think it's more important for us to seek and do it as well?*

_____

✳ *How do you think a person finds out God's will for his life?* _____

_____

Here Are Some Logical Steps...

...revealed in Scripture which you can go through so that you might find out what God's will is for your life.

I. *Realize that God __does have__ a will for your life.*

Since God is so in love with us He wishes to be involved in every possible detail of our lives. The things that happen to us moment by moment are very important to God.

Matthew 6:26
"Look at the birds of the air, that they do not sow, neither do they reap, nor gather into barns; and yet your heavenly Father feeds them. Are you not worth much more than they?"

✳ How much detailed concern do you think it takes to watch over and feed all the birds of the earth? _____

_____

> Since God is concerned about birds, doesn't it make sense that He would be more concerned about us, whom He loves?

Psalm 32:8
"I will instruct you and teach you in the way which you should go; I will counsel you with My eye upon you."

✳ To the person who wants God's will in a certain matter, what does God say? _____

_____

✳ How much do you think God's eye can see? _____

_____

God Makes The Point even Clearer!

Proverbs 3:5-6
"Trust in the Lord with all your heart, And do not lean on your own understanding. In all your ways acknowledge Him, And He will make your paths straight."

✳ Would God ask us to trust Him completely if He was going to let us down along the way? _____

✳ What does "He will make your paths straight" mean to you? _____

_____

19

God is not playing hide and go seek with us in connection with discovering His will. He doesn't put His will for us in a box and hide it behind a bush, saying, "Now go find it; I'll tell you when you're getting close." God does not ever play any kind of game with us.

✳✳ *If you want to know God's will, you must have an attitude of acceptance of His ways and His plans.*

> *In seeking God's will, one must do some deep soul-searching to discern one's own true motives. The question worth asking is, "Am I choosing only to do the part of God's will that I want to do and ignoring the rest?"*

A. GOD'S WILL IS STATED IN ROMANS...

Romans 12:1-2

(1) *"I urge you therefore, brethren, by the mercies of God, to present your bodies a living and holy sacrifice, acceptable to God, which*
(2) *is your spiritual service of worship. And do not be conformed to this world, but be transformed by the renewing of your mind, that you may prove what the will of God is, that which is good and acceptable and perfect."*

✳ *According to verse 1, we are to present ourselves a "living and holy sacrifice" to God. What do you think a "living and holy sacrifice" is?* _____

_____

*According to verse 2, what will we be able to prove if our lives are on God's altar? _____

_____

_____

¡IMPORTANT!

Unless our lives are in total submission and obedience to God and His ways, we are not in God's will, and we'll be confused about His plan for our lives. We can be confident, however, that if we are obedient to God, we are in His will.

B. HERE ARE TWO TESTS TO SEE IF WE HAVE THE RIGHT ATTITUDE TO BE IN GOD'S WILL.

First: Are you obeying the part of God's will that you already know is true?

In seeking God's will, it is foolish for us to seek it <u>only</u> in some vague parts of our lives. God's will is very complete, so we must be willing to obey <u>all</u> of it that He has already revealed to us. It won't do us any good to choose to ignore what we already know to be the thing He wants, but turn around and ask Him for clear direction about something else we want Him to show us.

FOR EXAMPLE...

A. God wants us to pray; not to pray as we ought to is to·be out of His will for us. (I Thessalonians 5:17)

B. God wants us to love each other; to have an unloving attitude constantly is to be out of God's will. (John 13:34-35)

C. It is God's will to spend time in the Bible; to spend little or no time in the Bible is clearly out of God's will. (II Timothy 3:16-17)

D. It is God's will that we are not run over by misused passion. If we are letting passion take control of our lives, we are out of God's will. (I Thessalonians 4:3-5)

Not to be in submission to the will of God, as already revealed, is to grieve Jesus Christ--Who is the One Who guides us into the will of God. *This is like stepping on the gas pedal and the brake pedal at the same time!*

John 14:21
"He who has My commandments and keeps them, he it is who loves Me; and he who loves Me shall be loved by My Father, and I will love him, and will disclose Myself to him."

AN EXPERIMENT...

Here is an experiment to see how you are doing in the matter of obedience to God's revealed will:

- *Make a list of all the habits and patterns of your daily schedule.*

- *Now go back over your list, and, next to each item, write either God's will or my will. (Realize that your will and God's will may in some instances be the same.)*

SAMPLE ACTIVITIES:

1 - sleeping till noon (my will)
2 - talking to my brothers and sisters (God's will)
3 - reading the Bible (God's will)
4 - one hour in front of mirror getting ready
     for school (my will)
5 - dating a Christian of the opposite sex (God's
     will and my will)
6 - having the heavy make-out scene (my will)
7 - three hours in front of TV (my will)

SECOND: *Are you willing to accept God's will for your life even before you know what it is?*

Mark 8:34-35
"And He summoned the multitude with His disciples, and said to them, 'If anyone wishes to come after Me, let him deny himself, and take up his cross, and follow Me. For whoever wishes to save his life shall lose it; and whoever loses his life for My sake and the gospel's shall save it."

✳ *What does it mean to deny yourself?* _____

_____

✳ *What does it mean to deny yourself with respect to the future?* _____

_____

_____

The truly dedicated Christian totally trusts his future into the hands of God, knowing that God's will is by far the best. His mind is already made up concerning the matter of following God wherever He may lead.

It is not pleasing to God to pray, "O God, show me your will for my life," while in the back of your mind you are thinking, "Show me your will so I can decide on whether or not I want to follow it."

WHEN WE HAVE DOUBTS...

...about whether or not we will follow God's will, we are telling Him that His love and wisdom isn't worth anything--which is an insult.

Romans 8:32
"He Who did not spare His own Son, but delivered Him up for us all, how will He not also with Him freely give us all things?"

✳ How much do you think it cost God to send Christ to die for us?

_____

✳ If He loved us enough to send Christ to die for us when we didn't care about Him, do you think that He will now play harmful little games with the rest of our lives? _____

III. REALIZE THAT A LARGE PART OF GOD'S PLAN FOR OUR LIVES IS ALREADY REVEALED FOR US IN THE BIBLE.

A. There are _two_ _different_ _aspects_ to God's will:

ONE: There is the part of His will for specific areas of our lives where God does not give specific instructions. For example, the school you should go to, the person to marry, job to have, etc.

TWO: There is the part of His will that applies to all Christians that is _specifically_ revealed in the Bible.

IMPORTANT !

We need to see that the majority of God's will is already revealed in the Bible and that you will waste a lot of time and emotional effort asking God for His will to be put forth when He has already done so in the Bible.

FOUR EXAMPLES OF HIS REVEALED WILL:

A. If you're asking if you should accept Christ, wondering whether it's God's will, this is absolutely silly. The Bible clearly tells us that God desires all men to come to Christ and accept Him as Saviour and Lord.

I Timothy 2:3-4
"This is good and acceptable in the sight of God our Saviour, who desires all men to be saved and to come to the knowledge of the truth."

B. If you're wondering whether you should obey your parents, don't wonder--obey.

Ephesians 6:1-2
"Children, obey your parents in the Lord, for this is right. Honor your father and mother (which is the first commandment with a promise).

C. If you're asking the question, "I wonder if I should share Christ with my neighbor?", don't wonder--do it.

Matthew 28:19-20
"Go therefore and make disciples of all the nations, baptizing them in the name of the Father and the Son and the Holy Spirit, teaching them to observe all that I commanded you; and lo, I am with you always, even to the end of the age."

D. Have you ever wondered whether God wants you to marry someone who doesn't know Jesus Christ as Lord and Saviour? Well don't wonder--He doesn't want you to ever do that!

II Corinthians 6:14-15
"Do not be bound together with unbelievers; for what partnership have righteousness and lawlessness, or what fellowship has light with darkness? Or what harmony has Christ with Belial, or what has a believer in common with an unbeliever?"

E. You might ask, "I wonder if God wants me to have this heavy make-out scene?"

I Thessalonians 4:3
"For this is the will of God, your sanctification; that is, that you abstain from sexual immorality."

CHECK iT OuT !

Before moving on to the next step in knowing God's will, see whether or not your particular question is already answered in the Bible. (Use a concordance study guide or fellow Christian for the answer to that question.)

If your question on God's will concerns an area of life that isn't specifically covered in the Scriptures, then you're ready for the next step.

IV. WHILE IT IS TRUE THAT GOD IS DEEPLY CONCERNED ABOUT US AND ABOUT REVEALING HIS WILL FOR OUR LIVES, THERE ARE SOME ASPECTS OF HIS PLAN THAT HE WILL ONLY REVEAL ONE DAY AT A TIME.

Most people think God will reveal His total will to them. They get frustrated when God only shows them a small percentage of the "blueprint" daily.

✳ Why is it that God reveals some of His will for our lives a little at a time? _____

_____

JESUS WAS TELLING HIS DISCIPLES...

...as they followed Him, of the future plan God had mapped out for them; but then he stopped and said:

John 16:12
"I have many more things to say to you, but you cannot bear them now."

Many people are not ready, emotionally and spiritually, to do what God wants of them down the road of life. They need to mature in faith, love, openness, etc. God not only reveals His moment by moment plan for us, but He uses life situations to prepare us for His future plan.

If God told us everything about our future, it would really burden us down today. This would make it nearly impossible for us to function as we should.

GOD HATES IT...

...when we worry about the future, since He wants us to just be concerned for today and His power for us today.

Matthew 6:34
"Therefore, do not be anxious for tomorrow; for tomorrow will care for itself. Each day has enough trouble of its own."

✳ According to the above verse, what remedies does God give us to prevent us from becoming anxious over tomorrow and the days after?

_____

YOU CAN TRUST GOD!

God thinks that it is very important that we wait on him and trust Him for everything. If we completely knew or even understood God's plan for our future, it would be every easy for us to quit seeking God with earnestness. We would focus more on the plan than on Him!

Psalm 27:14
"Wait for the Lord; Be strong, and let your heart take courage; Yes, wait for the Lord."

✱. *Do you think you would learn to trust God more by seeing Him work in your life after waiting in prayer, or by seeing Him work but knowing all along what He was going to do?* _____

_____

V. *YOU MUST REALIZE THAT GOD DIRECTS US TO HIS WILL THROUGH PRAYER.*

There is no greater time for God to gain access to our thoughts than when we are involved in deep serious prayer. So, as we have a desire for God to reveal His will to us, it is very important that we spend much time in prayer.

A. *Jesus Christ asked for the Father's will in His prayers.*

When Jesus was teaching His disciples to pray, He gave a sample prayer, which included the words:

Matthew 6:10
"Thy kingdom come,
Thy will be done,
On earth as it is in heaven."

✱ *Do you think Jesus had a part in the Father's will being done?* _____

_____

✱. *How do you think Jesus became aware of the Father's will?* _____

_____

When Jesus Christ had big decisions to make, which involved knowing God's will, He prayed.

Luke 6:12-13
(12)"And it was at this time that He went off to the mountain to pray, and He spent the whole night in prayer to God. And when day came,
(13)He called His disciples to Him, and chose twelve of them, whom He also named as apostles."

✳ What decision did Jesus make after the night of prayer? _____

_____

✳ Do you think Jesus asked for the Father's will concerning the choosing of the twelve when He prayed to the Father the night before? _____

Matthew 26:38-39
"Then He said to them (the disciples), 'My soul is deeply grieved, to the point of death; remain here and keep watch with me.' And he went a little beyond them, and fell on His face and prayed, saying, 'My Father, if it is possible, let this cup pass from Me; yet not as I will, but as Thou wilt."

✳ What was the great cry of Christ as He prayed? _____

_____

✳ What did "the cup" represent? _____

_____

Jesus Faced His Crisis With Prayer
When Jesus Christ was faced with making the decision that would take His life, He prayed. He prayed for the will of the Father. God's will was for Jesus Christ to die--that we might live!

The Important Thing To Remember...
...is that Jesus Christ prayed when He wanted to know the Father's will.

B. When the 1st Century church wanted to know God's will, they prayed.

Acts 13:2-3
"One day as these men were worshiping and fasting the Holy Spirit said, 'Dedicate Barnabas and Paul for a special job I have for them.' So after more fasting and prayer, the men laid their hands on them and sent them on their way."

✳ *What were the men doing when they received the will of God through the Holy Spirit?* __Praying__

GOD GOT THROUGH!
While the men were praying, the Holy Spirit had access to their thoughts. This allowed God the freedom to make His will known at that point in time.

C. *The Apostle Paul gives us a practical bit of instruction as He says:*

I Thessalonians 5:17
"Pray without ceasing."

✳ *What type of prayer is Paul speaking of?* _____

_____

PRAYER IS THE KEY
We can see from Christ's and the early church's example that prayer is an important key in helping us find the will of God.

LET'S EVALUATE THESE PRINCIPLES...
✳ *How much time have you spent in prayer seeking to know God's will for any area of your life?* _____

SPEND FIVE MINUTES

Sit down with some paper and a pencil and list specific areas in your life where you want God to reveal His will. Try spending five minutes a day praying about these same specific areas. You may want the help of a Christian friend who will meet daily with you to help with this. In doing this, <u>see how that you will both soon be two eye-witnesses to God showing you His will through prayer.</u>

VI. *TO DISCERN GOD'S WILL FOR LIFE'S SITUATIONS, IT IS WISE TO GET COUNSEL FROM THOSE WHO LOVE US AND ARE ACTIVELY SEEKING GOD'S WILL FOR THEIR OWN LIVES.*

A. *Problems of impulsiveness:*

DECISION ROAD

Feelings are a powerful and wonderful part of our psychological make-up, but it is easy for us to let our emotions act too quickly or impulsively about some decisions.

B. <u>*God uses other Christians as advisors, fact givers, and emotional balancers to perform His work, and to guide us to His will for us.*</u>

Proverbs 11:14
"Where there is no guidance, the people fall, But in abundance of counselors there is victory."

✳ *How is it that we can make a wrong decision without proper counsel?*

_____

EMOTIONS

GOD'S PEOPLE

DECISION ROAD

✳ Why is it that God wants us to have many counselors?_____

_____

6. _Seeking wise counsellors:_

Psalm 1:1
"How blessed is the man who does not walk in the counsel of the wicked,
Nor stand in the path of sinners, nor sit in the seat of scoffers!"

✳ Why do you think God wants us to put the greatest emphasis on the
counsel of those who are actively seeking God's will for their lives?

_____

_____

┌─────────────────────────────────────┐
│   WARNING!   │
│   If you feel strongly about a   │
│   decision you're about to make   │
│   but refuse to seek counsel on   │
│   it because of what others   │
│   may tell you, _you're making a_   │
│   _big mistake!_   │
└─────────────────────────────────────┘

Proverbs 12:15
"The way of a fool is right in his own eyes, But a wise man is he
who listens to counsel."

VII. THERE ARE TIMES WHEN GOD CAN USE CIRCUMSTANCES TO POINT US IN
THE DIRECTION WE SHOULD GO.

This was true in Paul's life...

Romans 1:13
"And I do not want you to be unaware, brethren, that often I have
planned to come to you (and have been prevented thus far) in order
that I might obtain some fruit among you also, even as among the
rest of the Gentiles."

*(Although Paul wanted to go see this Roman friend, God allowed some
circumstances to enter Paul's life which caused him to do other things
in a different location. Such circumstances as jail and overwhelming
spiritual needs in other places and distances were most likely used
to put Paul on God's course.)*

I Corinthians 16:8-9
(8)"But I shall remain in Ephesus until Pentecost; for a wide door for
(9)effective service has opened to me, and there are many adversaries."

✳ *Paul was writing to the people at Corinth to tell them what God had
shown him to do for the next several months. What circumstances did
Paul see that caused him to stay at Ephesus?* _____

_____

ANOTHER WARNING!

*It is easy to take circumstances and place
too heavy an emphasis on them because they
are so easy to see.*

*For example: When Jesus was going to the cross,
the circumstances were not too encouraging for
Him to continue. There were the circumstances
of pain, rejection and death--all telling Him
to stop. But there were other factors to consider. The other factors were that the Father
had revealed (in the Old Testament) that Christ
would die this kind of death and that the Holy
Spirit had borne witness with His Spirit that
He was the Christ and had to die for the sin of
mankind.*

*Be very careful how you "read" the circumstances
around you.*

*Let's say you
want to be a
doctor. You
apply for a
medical school,
but you are
turned down. It
would seem clear
at this point that
God is not leading
you to medical school.
On the other hand, if you are
accepted at four medical schools,
this doesn't necessarily mean that
God wants you in medical school.
There are other important factors
to consider beside the circumstances.*

WRAPPiNG iT UP...

In seeking God's will, be attentive to the circumstances.
But don't let them totally govern your particular decision in
determining His will.

• *If you are confident* God has a will for your life,

• *If you have committed* your life to obey what He has already revealed,

• *If you are determined* to follow whatever He has for you in the future,

• *If you have studied* the Word to find His will for your questions,

• *If you have sought counsel* from mature Christians,

• *If you have checked* the circumstances out thoroughly,

• *And if you have done some logical thinking,*

THEN MOVE AHEAD, DOING WHAT YOU SENSE IS THE BEST THING TO DO!

VIII. *ONCE OUR REBELLIOUS NATURE HAS COME UNDER SUBMISSION TO*
JESUS CHRIST AND WE ARE CONTROLLED AND EMPOWERED BY THE
HOLY SPIRIT, WE CAN ACCEPT BY FAITH THE FACT THAT OUR
REASONING IN THE MATTER IS SOUND, AND IS LED BY GOD.

II Timothy 1:7
"For God has not given us the spirit of timidity, but of power
and love and discipline (or sound judgment)."

GoD WANTS YoU To uSe YoUR MiND!
(after it is under His control)

You may need to get out a sheet of paper, and put down
the decision you need to make and the pros and cons so
you can see your alternatives plainly and clearly. The
alternatives will help you make your decision, when a
comparison can be made. At the top of the paper put
these words: "Which of these alternatives will bring
the most glory to Jesus Christ?"

1. Decision on what school I should attend.

Bible Belt University		Local Christian school	
PRO	CON	PRO	CON
1.		1.	
2.		2.	
3.		3.	
4.		4.	

NOW, BY SHEER TRUST, MOVE TOWARD YOUR DECISION...

By faith accept the following verses:

Philippians 2:13
"For it is God Who is at work in you both to will and to work for His good pleasure."

✳ *If you are committed to God--and He has promised to be at work in you to help you make the decision--Do you think that He will allow you to make a wrong decision?* _____

By faith, accept the fact that God will stop the wrong decision you might be making before damage is done. Knowing this must not make us go ahead and make any decision we want to--because we can never fool God about our efforts, our motives, or about anything else!

Psalm 37:23-24
(23)"The steps of a man are established by the Lord And He delights in his way. When he falls,,
(24) he shall not be hurled headlong; Because the Lord is the One who holds his hand."

GOD

✳ *In the above verses, Who is the One Who is actively involved in the man's situation?* _____

✳ *According to verse 24, what does God do to assure us that our decision will not lead us off a cliff to disaster?* _____

_____

BACK TO YOUR DECISION...

● *By faith, accept the idea that what you now want to do is also what God wants to do.*

● *Don't feel guilty about having a desire for a particular answer.*

Psalm 37:4-5
(4)"Delight yourself in the Lord And He will give you the desires of
(5) your heart. Commit your way to the Lord; Trust also in Him and He will do it."

34

GO FOR iT !

God is happy when you are happy in His will! Don't feel guilty about your desires if they are Godly ones! God loves to give good gifts as long as those gifts don't become "gods" in our lives.

In a phrase, "GO FOR IT," and move towards a decision. Be ready to move!

Ecclesiastes 11:4 (Living Bible)
"If you wait for perfect conditions, you will never get anything done."

NOTES

The importance of a balanced
SELF-IMAGE
Discussion 3

HERE ARE SOME
QUESTIONS TO PONDER...

✳ *What do you think of yourself?*

✳ *Do you accept yourself just as you are, or would you like to be more like someone else?*

✳ *Has "nature given you the shaft" by allowing you a not-too-good-looking face or body?*

✳ *Do you hate the way you look?*

✳ *Do you feel that you could be better off socially or materially if you were a little better looking?*

✳ *Do you think God should have given you more abilities?*

Beginning to Take Stock of Yourself...

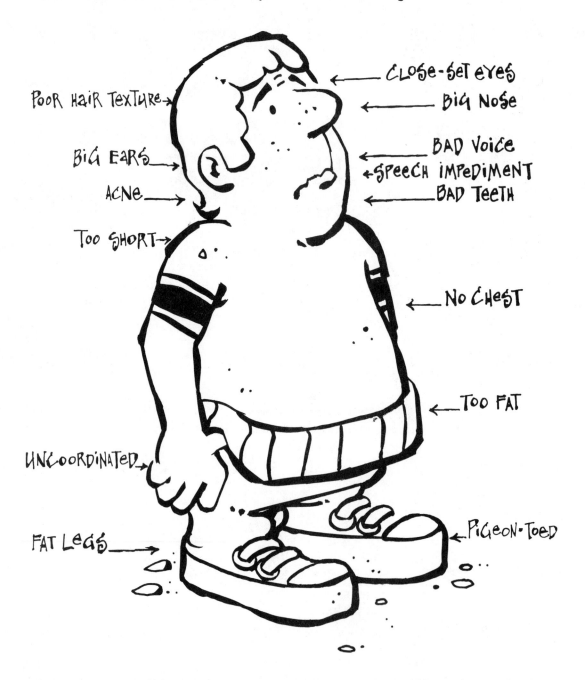

HERE IS A LIST OF WHAT SEEM TO BE PHYSICAL SHORTCOMINGS THAT MIGHT
AFFECT US IN THE WAYS WE ACCEPT OURSELVES AND THE GOD WHO MADE US
(Be it ever so painful, please pick out some that pertain to you):

●too fat	●bad voice	●no chest	●scars
●too short	●big feet	●deformed	●impediment
●too tall	●fat legs	●acne	●poor eyes
●big nose	●skinny legs	●big ears	●bad teeth
●uncoordinated	●close-set eyes	●pigeon-toed	●poor hair-texture
●bowed legs	●_____	●_____	●_____

"THANKS ALOT, GOD."

It's easy for us to look in the mirror and say to ourselves, "Thanks alot, God, for nothing; You sure blew it when You came to me. I'll take over from now on when it comes to me, if You don't mind. Your kind of creativity I don't need."

While we may not really say this, down deep in our inner selves we may sense it.

If you have a poor attitude toward accepting yourself, it can affect your relationships with:

OTHERS ___ *No one likes to be around a person who is always criticizing himself.*

YOURSELF ___ *It's not enjoyable to be unhappy about yourself.*

GOD ___ *It's hard to trust God in other areas of your life if you feel He hasn't been too smart in how He made you.*

IN THIS TIME TOGETHER...

...let's answer some important questions:

✱ *Why are we affected so greatly by our abilities and physical appearance?*

_____

_____

✱ *How can we learn to have a healthy acceptance of ourselves in the future?*

_____

_____

41

I. *THE REASON WE ARE SO DEEPLY AFFECTED BY OUR OWN ABILITIES AND GOOD LOOKS IS BECAUSE <u>THE WORLD WE LIVE IN IS ALL CAUGHT UP IN BEAUTY AND ABILITY</u>, AND WE AS CHRISTIANS CAN GET INVOLVED IN THIS MESS.*

ASK YOURSELF THESE QUESTIONS.

1. *<u>Who gets more attention</u> in life, the pretty baby or the ugly baby?*

2. *<u>Who wins scholarships</u> at baby contests, the pretty baby or the ugly baby?*

3. *<u>Who gets kidded</u> about the way he looks --an attractive 5-year-old or an ugly 5-year-old?*

4. *<u>Who is more likely to get the benefit</u> of the doubt on a borderline grading situation in school--the attractive girl or the ugly girl?*

5. *<u>Who gets the dates?</u> All things being equal in areas except physical appearance, <u>who has the most friends?</u>*

6. *<u>Who is more likely to be student body president?</u>*

7. *<u>Who is more likely to get a job?</u>*

8. *<u>Who is more likely to have confidence?</u>*

THE WORLD'S POINT OF VIEW

It becomes evident that, from the world's perspective, one can usually find more advantages in being thought to be physically attractive. From the world's viewpoint, this will lead directly to more success, acceptance and general happiness.

A. *<u>It is wise to understand that the big value put on appearance (looks, body, clothes) is part of a thought-system that is hostile to God and His ways</u>.*

✱ *Why do you think that man, apart from God, seems to put so much emphasis on appearance? _____*

Ephesians 4:17-19
(17)This I say therefore, and affirm together with the Lord, that you walk no longer just as the Gentiles walk, in the futility of their
(18)mind, being darkened in their understanding, excluded from the life of God, because of the ignorance that is in them, because of the
(19)hardness of their heart; and they, having become callous, have given themselves over to sensuality, for the practice of every kind of impurity with greediness."

✱ *According to verse 17, where has the wrong set of values led those who ignore God? _____*

_____

✱ What does, "being darkened in their understanding, excluded from the life of God" mean? _____

_____

_____

✱ According to verse 19, what has happened to the godless man? _____

_____

_____

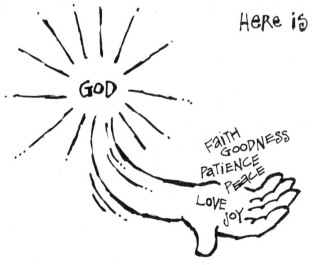

As a man hardens his heart toward God, he cuts himself off from understanding true beauty as God sees it. So being cut off, man turns to the mere superficial--not to true inner beauty as shown in beauty as shown in love, kindness, gentleness, joy, quietness, and patience which comes from within-- but to that which is external.

MAN HAS TURNED...

...to almost total concentration on sex, body, physical strength, alluring clothes, and looks. In short, he has turned to his glands.

Here is WHAT is HAPPENING AROUND US:

God's counsel gives us true values, and beauty that is inside a man or woman--glowing inner spiritual beauty which, in the true Christian, reflects God Himself.

GOD

FaiTH GOODNESS PATIENCE PEACE LOVE JOY

BUT MAN...

...*ignoring God and His ways, doesn't understand what true beauty is, and makes up his own rules to beauty.* <u>*Beauty to natural man is mere sensuality.*</u>

Now man, with these twisted values, puts prime importance on how a person looks. "Beauty" is all important. If you are ugly or even less attractive physically, you don't make it in this system.

YOU JUST CAN'T CUT IT!

Trying to look just right--sensual, well-built physically, perfectly dressed--will lead eventually to frustration. No person, because of age, can stay handsome or beautiful for very long. Styles and "taste" change too rapidly and are very hard to keep up with.

SO DON'T GET CAUGHT UP IN THE DEAD-END RAT-RACE!

<u>*You, as a Christian, aren't supposed to get caught up in the "wrong values on outward appearance"; in fact, it's a sin to do this. God doesn't want you to be "conformed" to that kind of thinking, since it always leads to frustration and failure and cuts right across His will for you and for other believers. He wants inner beauty!*</u>

Romans 12:2
"And do not be conformed to this world, but be transformed by the renewing of your mind, that you may prove what the will of God is, that which is good and acceptable and perfect."

II. *WE CAN COME TO HAVE A MUCH HEALTHIER VIEW OF OURSELVES IF WE LOOK AT OUR APPEARANCE AND ABILITIES THE WAY GOD LOOKS AT THEM.*

Here are six different ways that God views you and your self-acceptance.

1. *God does not put prime importance on physical appearance and strength.*

I Samuel 16:7
"But the Lord said to Samuel, 'Do not look at his appearance or at the height of his stature, because I have rejected him; for God sees not as man sees, for man looks at the outward appearance, but the Lord looks at the heart.'"

✳ *Why does God put so much more importance on the inner man, rather than on just physical appearance?* _____

_____

These ANSWERS ARE IMPORTANT!

1. *Man's frame (physical body) is only a temporary item.* *It weakens and dies with the passing of time; yet, man's inward personality, the soul, will live on forever.*

2. *The physical frame has great limitation, as far as change goes. Man, when he is born, is limited in his ability to change the basic aspects of his physical body. Man does, however, have an ability to change and develop his inward personality and character. God sees this type of inward development as being of much greater importance than the physical.*

45

THAT'S WHY GOD SAYS:

Proverbs 31:30
"Charm is deceitful and beauty is vain, But a woman who fears the Lord, she shall be praised."

＊ Why is it that the use of appearance to allure someone is deceitful?

_____

_____

＊ Why is physical beauty vain? _____

_____

WARNING!

Anybody who trusts in physical beauty to carry them through life walks on very thin ice. Beauty fades quickly, proving that <u>our body begins to die</u> even as we are born, and that physical degeneration sets in in our twenties.

PHYSICAL BEAUTY

God is not overwhelmed by one's physical strength either:

Psalm 147:10-11
(10)"He does not delight in the strength of the horse; He does not take
(11)pleasure in the legs of a man. The Lord favors those who fear Him, Those who wait for his lovingkindness."

＊. Why do you think God is not overwhelmed by man's strength?_____

_____

iT'S OBVioUS!

It has become obvious that God does not want us to have <u>undue</u> worry about our appearance, to concern ourselves with just the right clothes. Jesus also made this clear while teaching His disciples.

Matthew 6:28-29
"And why are you anxious about clothing? Observe how the lilies of the field grow; they do not toil nor do they spin, yet I say to you that even Solomon in all his glory did not clothe himself like one of these."

2. <u>Realizing that God does not focus on the external, we need to understand that He does focus on the inner person. His desire for us is to have real inner beauty.</u>

iT'S HARDER To GeT, BUT BeTTeR To HaVe

While true inner beauty is much more difficult to achieve, and is less appealing to a world with the erotic on its mind, it nonetheless will make both us and God happy for all eternity.

WHaT i$ iNNeR BeaUTY?

It is the inner character that the Holy Spirit develops within Christians that pleases God. It involves peace, patience, kindness, goodness, gentleness, faithfulness, love, joy, and self-control.

I Peter 3:3-4
"And let not your adornment be external only--braiding the hair, and wearing gold jewelry, and putting on dresses; but let it be the hidden person of the heart, with the imperishable quality of a <u>gentle</u> and <u>quiet</u> spirit which is <u>precious</u> in the sight of God."

※ What two imperishable qualities does God desire to develop within a girl's life? _____

✳ How does God view these qualities? _____

✳ Does a girl have to be good-looking or well-shaped to have these qualities?

_____

Isaiah 40:30-31
(30)"Though _youths_ grow weary and tired, and _vigorous_ young men stumble
(31)badly, Yet _those who wait for the Lord_ will gain new strength; They
    will mount up with wings like eagles, They will run and not get
    tired, They will walk and not become weary."

✳ In verse 30, what two attributes are mentioned that our society
  greatly values? _____

✳ According to verse 31, what inner quality does God respond to?

_____

GOD IS KEEPING SCORE

It would be wise for us to spend more time and
emotional energy developing the inner beauty
that God counts valuable rather than worrying
over the world's way of boosting the self-image
by living for appearance, ending in frustration.

---

3. God wants us to realize that He was
   actively involved in the creation of
   our bodies, making them for His own
   purposes, and that He is still
   participating in their development.

Psalm 139:13-15
(13)"For Thou didst form my inward parts;
    Thou didst weave me in my mother's womb.
(14)I will give thanks to Thee, for I am fear-
    fully and wonderfully made; Wonderful are
    Thy works, And my soul knows it very well.
(15)My frame was not hidden from Thee, When I was made
    in secret, And skillfully wrought in the depths of the
    earth."

✳ When did God become involved in your appearance? _____

_____

✳ According to verse 15, does it appear that God haphazardly throws man
  together? _____

Ephesians 2:10
"For we are His workmanship, created in Christ Jesus for good works, which God prepared beforehand, that we should walk in them."

GOD IS THE MASTER DESIGNER

God is deeply concerned that people look at us and think of Him. He is also concerned that men come to know Jesus Christ. Therefore, He designs our frame so that through us, when we are His and are living in the power of the Holy Spirit, He (God) will receive glory, and people will come to know Christ.

God made our bodies and is still actively involved in developing them for the work He has for us that will bring glory to Him. Do you think it would be wise to thank Him for the frame we have, and trust Him to continue His work in and through us?

4. *God wants us to realize the importance of having a healthy countenance.*

LET'S DEFINE COUNTENANCE:

> *"Countenance is the expression of the face which reveals the inner condition of the heart."*

Psalm 43:5
"Why art thou cast down, O my soul? And why art thou disquieted within me? Hope in God, for I shall yet praise Him, Who is the health of my countenance, and my God."

✻ *According to verse 5, what was the condition of David's soul?*

_____

✻ *Even though David's soul was full of anxiety, what did he expect to happen in the near future?* _____

✻ *What do you think was the key to the health of David's countenance?*

_____

HERE IS THE KEY...

The key is found in David's relationship with God. The health of David's countenance came as a reward for his trust and hope in the God he loved and praised.

A. Let's consider those things which can prevent us from having a healthy countenance.

We've already stated that a person's countenance is their facial expression, which reveals the inner condition of the heart. A <u>healthy</u> countenance is one that is based on a heart that is trusting in God, and this trust and faith in God is reflected through the outward expression of a person's face. <u>A truly healthy countenance can't be faked or acted.</u>

Proverbs 25:23
"The north wind brings forth rain, and a backbiting tongue, an angry countenance."

✳ What type of a reaction do you have when you know someone is talking against you behind your back? _____

_____

✳ *How does anger effect your countenance?* _____

_____

```
┌─────────────────────────────────────────────────┐
│                   A PROJECT!                      │
│  The next time you get angry, before you do or say│
│  anything that you'll regret, go and look at your │
│  eyes, your face and just your overall appearance │
│  in a mirror.                                     │
└─────────────────────────────────────────────────┘
```

```
┌─────────────────────────────────────────────────┐
│               ANOTHER PROJECT!                    │
│  Or, the next time you notice someone becoming    │
│  angry, see if their countenance changes visibly. │
└─────────────────────────────────────────────────┘
```

ITS EASY TO SEE...

...that anger does not really bring out the best in a person. That's why James 1:20 says, "For the anger of man does not achieve the righteousness of God."

SIN CAN OFTEN BE THE CAUSE OF AN UNHEALTHY COUNTENANCE!

(We see this often in the lives and faces of those who don't know God.)

Isaiah 3:9
"The expression of their faces bears witness against them. And they display their sin like Sodom; They do not even conceal it. Woe to them!"

✳ *As people live in open rebellion from God and His will, what part of their appearance bears witness that they are rebelling?* _____

_____

The countenance of many people who don't know God often reveals the emptiness and sinfulness of their own hearts.

David knew this as he said in Psalm 10:4, "The wicked in the haughtiness of his countenance, does not seek Him; all his thoughts are, 'There is no God.'"

UNCONFESSED SIN...

...*can also greatly affect the countenance of a person who loves God.*

Psalm 32:3-4
"When I kept silent about my sin, my body wasted away Through my groaning all day long. For day and night Thy hand was heavy upon me; my vitality was drained away as with the fever-heat of summer."

✳ *David had committed a great sin before God; from verses 4 & 5, what were the results of not confessing his sin?* _____

_____

> # UNCONFESSED SIN WILL COST YOU!
>
> *Unconfessed sin has a tremendous effect upon the health of our physical body. David's entire physical countenance was greatly disturbed as a result of his unconfessed sin, and we are built the same way he was.*

D. *Now let's take a look at those things which can contribute to us having a healthy countenance.*

REALIZING THAT UNCONFESSED SIN CAN CAUSE AN UNHEALTHY COUNTENANCE...
...the first thing for us to do is to confess all *known sin to God.*

I John 1:9
"If we confess our sins, He is faithful and righteous to forgive us our sins and to cleanse us from all unrighteousness."

✳ *What does it mean to confess our sin?* _____

_____

CONFESSION INVOLVES THREE THINGS.

- *agreeing with God that He was right and that what we did was wrong. (This is difficult, because we are proud.)*

- *agreeing with God that Christ paid for that sin in full at the cross.*

- *deciding, by an act of the will, that we will turn away from that wrong that so hurt God.*

✳ *When we confess our sins, according to verse 9, how much of our sin is forgiven?* _____

✳ *How much does "all" mean?* _____

CONFESSION BRINGS FREEDOM

All of us know what it is to carry the guilt of committing an offense toward God and others. Many of us know the tremendous lift of spirits that comes when we confess that sin and are completely forgiven. If we confess our offense to God, He completely forgives us and wipes away the guilt we have for committing the offense. Therefore, confession brings freedom from guilt, which will contribute to a healthy countenance.

ANOTHER IMPORTANT ITEM:

While it is true that all of our sin primarily offends and grieves God and need to be confessed before Him, it is also possible that our earthly relationships can be broken as a result of these offenses. Therefore, we need to be sensitive to others around us, so that if we offend them (as a result of our sin toward God), we need to go to them and ask them for forgiveness for our offense.

James tells us what will happen to that broken relationship if we confess our offense to the person we hurt:

James 5:16
"Therefore, confess your sins to one another, and pray for one another, so that you may be healed."

BEING FULLY FORGIVEN...

...now enables us to enter the presence of God, which contributes to our having a healthy countenance.

Psalm 34:5
"They looked to Him and were radiant, And their faces shall never be ashamed."

✳ What does "they looked to Him" mean? _____

_____

```
┌─────────────────────────────────────────────┐
│            MOMENT BY MOMENT                   │
│   It is very important for us to live each    │
│   day, moment by moment, with our vision      │
│   fixed on God. We have said that a healthy   │
│   heart will bring a healthy countenance.     │
│   As we look to God for all of our needs,     │
│   He causes us to have a countenance          │
│   that will bring glory to Him. (See          │
│   Hebrews 12:2-3; Acts 4:13)                  │
└─────────────────────────────────────────────┘
```

3. Being with close friends who love Jesus Christ and who desire to
bring honor to Him will contribute to a healthy countenance.
countenance.

Proverbs 27:17
"Iron sharpens iron, so one man sharpens another."
friend."

✳ What does it mean for someone's countenance
to be visibly sharp? _____

_____

_____

✳ How do you think the right friends
can enhance the health of your own
countenance? _____

_____

Hebrews 10:24-25
"...and let us consider how to stimulate one another to love and good
deeds, not forsaking our own assembling together, as is the habit of
some, but encouraging one another."

4. A joyful heart will also help elevate our countenance to health.

Proverbs 15:13
"A joyful heart makes a cheerful face (countenance), But when the
heart is sad, the spirit is broken."

✳ What brings about a joyful heart? _____

_____

54

A JOYFUL HEART...

...is brought about by understanding that God is in absolute control of your life if you allow Him to be--by faith. Jesus told His disciples:

John 14:1
"Let not your heart be troubled; believe in God, believe also in Me."

✳ What does it mean to have a troubled heart? _____

_____

REMEMBER...

To have a healthy countenance...

1. Confess all known sin
2. Spend time in God's presence
3. Spend time with close friends who love Jesus Christ
4. Let Jesus Christ have <u>complete</u> control of your heart.

---

5. <u>Still another key to overcoming a self-acceptance problem is to let what seems to be our weakness be a motivation to let God work through us all the more.</u>

If one abides by and compares himself to the world's standards of human worth, based on beauty and ability that rules out God and His ways, one will continue to have poor self-acceptance.

HOWEVER...

...if we keep this rule in mind, we can turn our inferiorities around and in God's power allow them to be a great help.

I Corinthians 1:27
"...but God has chosen the foolish things of the world to shame the wise, and God has chosen the weak things of the world to shame the things which are strong."

✳ *According to this verse, what two things does God use to show His greatness?* _____

WHAT ARE THE FOOLISH...	WHAT ARE THE WEAK...
...things in your life? *(as seen by the world)*	*...things in your life* *(as seen by the world)*
1) *not enough education* 2) *not enough money* 3) *very little rank (at school, job or other)* 4) *very little power* 5) *not too popular*	1) *little natural beauty* 2) *little physical strength* 3) *not real clever on how to get ahead in life by scheming, flattery, "white" lying or cheating* 4) *feeling too young*

BUT REMEMBER...

...that God has made it a rule of life to <u>lift</u> <u>up</u> <u>the</u> <u>very</u> <u>things</u> that godless people think are silly. (A classic example of this is our Lord Jesus Christ.)

LOOK AT THE MAN JESUS CHRIST

Jesus Christ seemingly moved in a weak and foolish way when he humbled Himself to become a man. Not only did He become a man, but He also seemed even weaker and more foolish when he wasn't physically all that attractive --in the world's sense of attractive.

Isaiah 53:2
"For He grew up before Him like a tender shoot And like a root out of parched ground. <u>He has no stately form or majesty</u> That we should look upon Him, <u>Nor appearance that we should be attracted to Him</u>."

✱ What are two physical attributes that seemed to be a negative for Christ--outwardly speaking? _____

_____

AND YET...

Jesus Christ rocked the world with power--the power He had as He walked and lived in His total dependance upon the Father. (see Matthew 28:18, John 7:46)

GETTING YOURSELF TOGETHER!

Here's how to make what you feel is your physical deficiency, or your handicap ability, usable to bring glory to God.

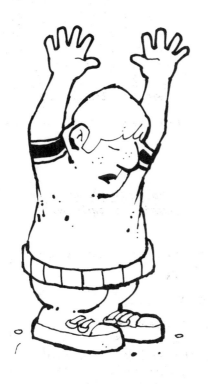

As you seek to serve God, pray a prayer something like this:

"Dear God, I know that by the world's standards I may not have all the beauty and the ability there is. Because this is true, I know I must trust You rather than any ability or appearance I have to get the job done. Now I trust You to use what appears to be a weakness as a great new strength for You. Thank You."

If you really pray a prayer something like this from your heart, and behave in this way as you walk with God in everyday living, you will be able to say this verse with great relevance to your life:

II Corinthians 12:10
"Therefore I am well content with weaknesses, with insults, with distresses, with persecutions, with difficulties, for Christ's sake; for when I am weak, then I am strong."

6. <u>We should realize how God desires us to view our abilities and talents.</u>

SOME OF US ARE EXTREMELY BEAUTIFUL...

...and physically gifted from the world's perspective. If you're
a Christian and do have talent or attractiveness of this kind, here's
a checklist to help you get a proper perspective on this:

- Is it valid to be a Christian and still be a professional
  athlete?

- What about being a cheerleader--is that wrong?

- Should I try to get all "A" grades if I'm smart?

(Have you ever wondered about these or similar questions?)

A. <u>We should realize just what there is in us which has true value.</u>

The Apostle Paul was a very gifted, intelligent man. He had excelled
in his life and position as a Pharisee. Let's see how he felt
concerning his accomplishments:

Philippians 3:4b-8
"If anyone else has a mind to put confidence in the flesh, I far more:
(5) circumcised the eighth day, of the nation of Israel, of the tribe of
Benjamin, a Hebrew of Hebrews; as to the Law, a Pharisee; as to zeal,
(6) a persecutor of the church; as to the righteousness which is in the Law,
(7) found blameless. But whatever things were gain to me, those things I
(8) have counted as loss for the sake of Christ. More than that, I count
all things to be loss in view of the surpassing value of knowing
Christ Jesus my Lord, for whom I have suffered the loss of all things,
and count them but rubbish in order that I may gain Christ."

✳ Verses 4 through 6 tell us of Paul's social and occupational position
in his day. He had excelled to reach the top, yet Paul tells us that
all he had and was couldn't even begin to compare to knowing one
Person. Who was that Person? _____

✳ Why did Paul consider knowing Christ of greater value than earthly
accomplishments? _____

_____

+---+
| IMPORTANT THOUGHT |
| |
| Paul had the proper perspective in relation to |
| the value of earthly abilities. We must first |
| understand that the most important thing in life|
| is our relationship with Christ. |
+---+

58

B. _Now that we've put our love and knowledge of Christ first, we can_
   be free to excel in every area of life for His glory.

Colossians 3:17
"And whatever you do in word or deed, do all in the name of the Lord
Jesus, giving thanks through Him to God the Father."

✳ _What does it mean to "do all in the name of the Lord Jesus Christ?"_

_____

_____

✳ _What should be your attitude as you use the abilities God has given_
   to you? _____

✳ _Why should you have a thankful heart?_

   _____

   _____

   _____

THUS WE SHOULD:

- _Remember that Christ is more important_
  than any ability or accomplishment that
  we could ever do

- _Use all your abilities to bring honor_
  and glory to Jesus Christ

THE BIG SUMMARY!

1. _God does not put prime importance on physical appearance_
   and strength.

2. _Realizing that God does not focus on the external, we need to_
   understand that He does focus on the inner person. His desire
   for us is to have real inner beauty.

3. _God wants us to realize that He was actively involved in the_
   creation of our bodies, making them for His own purposes, and
   that He is still participating in their development.

4. _God wants us to realize the importance of having a healthy countenance._

5. _We must let what seems to be our weakness be a motivation for letting God work through us all the more._

6. _We should realize how God desires us to view our abilities and our talents._

CONCLUSION...

Remember that John 3:16 says:
"For God so loved the world, that He gave His only begotten Son, that whoever believes in Him should not perish, but have eternal life."

You are part of the world into which God sent His Son, Jesus Christ. God's love for the people of the world motivated His to send Jesus. Isn't it great to know God feels that we are that important and valuable!?! God demonstrated just how important He knows we are. Now we also need to realize how important we are, giving ourselves back to Him for His loving purpose for us!

NOTES

The importance of dealing with
LONELINESS
DISCUSSION 4

NOW LET'S PRESENT...

<u>Loneliness</u>.

Loneliness is just about everyone's acquaintance, but no one's friend! It is one of the most crippling problems facing you in modern society.

WHAT IS LONELINESS?

- *<u>Loneliness</u> is having your closest friend miles away with no one else to share your pain or your joy*

- *<u>Loneliness</u> is missing a few days at school or work, and having no one notice*

- *<u>Loneliness</u> is that deep, hollow feeling that says, "My opinions aren't important to anyone."*

- *<u>Loneliness</u> is sitting alone at home on Friday night, knowing the special friend you'd like to date is out with someone else.*

- *<u>Loneliness</u> is the dread of going to the cafeteria and knowing there will be no one to sit with while you eat*

- *<u>Loneliness</u> is that gnawing feeling that few, if any, people really understand you*

- *<u>Loneliness</u> is wondering which of your "friends" are really friends, and which are just trying to use you.*

WHAT IS LONELINESS TO YOU?

✳ *Can you remember when you were the most lonely?*

✳ *Have you sensed loneliness in the last two weeks?*

Loneliness cuts down into some of the deepest needs you have. These needs include the overwhelming desire to love, to be loved, and to be held in high esteem by at least one other person.

When these deep needs are not satisfied, you can become almost paralyzed by a sort of suffocating feeling of frustration and helplessness. This is known by millions of people, and can be called <u>loneliness</u>.

Here Are Several Steps You Can Take...

...to discern loneliness and to deal with the agony of it in your life.

I *THE FIRST STEP OUT OF LONELINESS IS TO <u>STOP</u>, MENTALLY <u>GET HOLD OF YOURSELF</u>, THEN <u>MOVE AHEAD</u>.*

Feelings of loneliness are emotionally crippling, and can easily lead you into a vicious circle of frustration and helplessness. It is very important for you to realize whether or not you are caught in this circle of frustration.

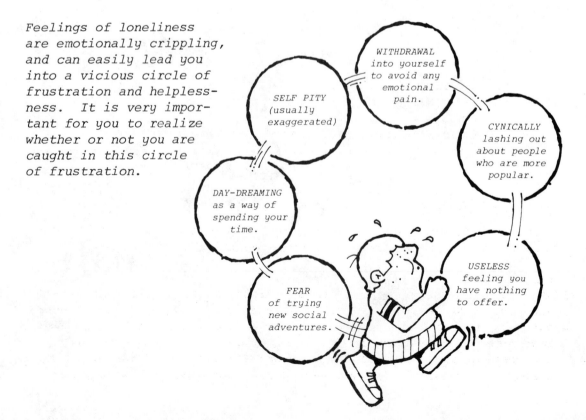

WITHDRAWAL
into yourself
to avoid any
emotional
pain.

SELF PITY
(usually
exaggerated)

CYNICALLY
lashing out
about people
who are more
popular.

DAY-DREAMING
as a way of
spending your
time.

USELESS
feeling you
have nothing
to offer.

FEAR
of trying
new social
adventures.

Here Are Some Symptoms...

...that will help you to detect
any loneliness you might be
experiencing:

- a sense of _self_ _pity_, thinking that no one really cares for you
  (this is usually an exaggeration)

- spending too much of your time _day-dreaming_

- _withdrawing_ yourself from others to avoid emotional pain

- becoming _cynical_ and sarcastic about other, more popular, people

- _fear_ of trying new social adventures

- feeling you are _useless_, having nothing to offer to anyone.

> SPENDING LARGE BLOCS OF TIME
> BEING EMOTIONALLY FRUSTRATED
> OR DRAINED IS NOT GOD'S PLAN
> OR DESIRE FOR US!

Matthew 11:28
"Come to Me, all who are weary and heavy laden, and I will give
you _rest_."

A. What is the one gift Christ wants to give you when you are
overwhelmed by the pressures and loneliness you face? _____

(Rest.)

B. If you are into the vicious circle of being upset mentally and
emotionally, are we experiencing that gift?

C. Do you think Christ would withhold the gift of rest (quiet
confidence) from you after promising to give it?

It is Possible...

...for you to get hold of these crippling emotions by following the
example of a man who shares his needs in this Psalm:

Psalm 42:3-5
(3) "My tears have been my food day and night, While they say to me all
day long, 'Where is your God?' These things I remember, and I pour
(4) out my soul within me. For I used to go along with the throng and
lead them in procession to the house of God, With the voice of joy
and thanksgiving, a multitude keeping festival. Why are you in
despair, O my soul? And why have you become disturbed within me?

(5)Hope in God, for I shall again praise Him for the help of His presence."

⋇ According to verses 3 and 4 in this Psalm, what were some of the circumstances that caused the man to be so emotionally upset and lonely? _____

_____

_____

⋇ According to verse 5 (and see also verse 11 for the total context), what did the Psalmist do to begin to see victory over his pained emotions? _____

_____

Now Here Are A Few Important Questions...

...or practical statements you may want to say to yourself when you find that you are in an emotional tailspin over loneliness:

"SELF, this crippling feeling of isolation is not helping me or pleasing God one bit. I must begin to act now to see real victory."

"SELF, in the power of Christ you are going to do the seemingly impossible, and break out of this slump of loneliness."

"SELF, while you are sitting here emotionally paralyzed, there are many people in need of your love. Find them."

"SELF, it's time you get the victory over circumstances that come your way, and over your own emotions."

II. THE SECOND STEP OUT OF LONELINESS IS TO BE HONEST WITH YOURSELF,
WITH GOD, AND WITH OTHERS.

TRUE HONESTY CAN BE PaiNFUL:

...because it proclaims life's situations the way they are, not the
way we'd like them to be.

A. First, we must be totally honest with ourselves. Once we have
gotten hold of ourselves, we must ask ourselves some very searching
questions, seeking some honest answers.

HERE ARE a FEW QUESTIONS WORTH ASKING...

✳ Does my hostility, caused by a strange reaction to loneliness,
drive other people away?

Proverbs 18:19
"A brother offended is harder to be won than a strong city,
And contentions are like the bars of a castle."

✳ Do I really want out of my loneliness?

✳ Do I show my thoughts of isolation by the expression on my face?

✳ Am I really unnecessarily afraid of people?

✳ If so, why am I afraid of them?

✳ Do I really believe God can help solve my loneliness problem?

✳ Am I willing to be hurt to love others?

✳ What is it I'm trying to protect by withdrawing? Is it working?
What are the consequences?

WE NEED EACH OTHER!

If you are a Christian, and you have been priding yourself on being the "Lone Ranger" in your affairs with others, you are clearly not in accord with the Scripture and the example of Jesus Christ.

Rather than being this way, you should have the attitude expressed in these verses:

Hebrews 10:24-25
(24) "And let us consider how to stimulate one another to love and good deeds,
(25) not forsaking our own assembling together, as is the habit of some, but encouraging one another; and all the more, as you see the day drawing near."

Romans 1:12 (Living Bible)
"Then, too, I need your help, for I want not only to share my faith with you but to be encouraged by yours: Each of us will be a blessing to the other."

YOU MUST BE WILLING TO SAY TO YOURSELF:

"Being a loner is not God's way. It's time I begin to open up to others."

B. It is important to be honest with God about our loneliness and our deepest needs. There is a tendency for us, when loneliness strikes, to not share our pains before God and therefore be dishonest toward Him. This is a big mistake! God wants our honesty. God says, in I Peter 5:7, "Casting all your anxiety upon Him, because He cares for you."

✳ What does "casting" mean? _____

✳ What are "anxieties?" _____

✳ What are some anxieties about loneliness that we can cast on Him?

_____

_____

_____

("*God, I know I have nothing to offer others. My best friends have misunderstood me. I'm not sure I can take this loneliness much longer. I seem to resent people who are at ease in a crowd. I may tell others my Christian life is together, but frankly, I'm miserable.*")

Be HONEST

God will never belittle you for being honest with Him about your deep inner feelings. He loves and cares for you.

JOB--AN EXAMPLE OF HONESTY TO GOD...

Job was a man who was deeply lonely due to suffering and misunderstanding by his closest friends. In his frustration and heartbreak, he dealt simply and openly with the God he loved.

Job 16:19-21
(19)"*Even now, behold, my witness is in heaven, And my advocate is on*
(20)*high. My friends are my scoffers; My eye weeps to God. O that a*
(21)*man might plead with God As a man with his neighbor!*"

ONCE YOU REALIZE YOU'RE LONELY...

...you need to be honest with God. God's ability to work in our lives is dependent upon our openness to Him, and our allowing Him to absorb our deep inner hurt. The more we are honest with Him, giving Him the freedom to handle our pain and fears through sharing them with Him, the more He will be able to aid in healing our loneliness.

C. *Honesty needs to be shown by being truthful with others as we share our hurt selves and seek their help. We tend not to seek counsel from others in the areas of loneliness and friendship because of the fear of looking weak and unspiritual. This attitude of fear of what others might think is self-defeating and goes against God's counsel.*

Ephesians 4:25
"*Therefore, laying aside falsehood, speak truth, each one of you with his neighbor, for we are members of one another.*"

✱ *Is it possible to tell a lie or live a lie before our brothers and sisters in Christ without using our words?* _____

Most of us have the idea that honestly sharing a need with a friend reveals personal weakness and emotional instability. We think the truly strong person "works it out" on his own or is able to "handle it" by himself.

This is not God's idea at all.

It really takes more courage, in most instances, to share with God and a friend that we are weak and need his help then it does to hold it in. Therefore, we should be honest with God and each other, and share our loneliness with close Christian friends who can counsel and help us thaw out of our isolation.

Fellow Christians have a capacity to meet our need of loneliness, and many times they _will_ help meet this need if we are honest and open...

IMPORTANT!

One reason God put a new life in Christians (those who submit their lives to God) is so they will realize their capacity to help others. They have not only the capacity to carry their own burdens, but the burdens of others as well.

Galatians 6:2
"Bear one another's burdens, and thus fulfill the law of Christ."

ASK GOD TO SHOW YOU...
...who the other Christians are who could counsel and help you.

✳ Can you think of someone who knows Christ, who you could really seek for help on this matter of loneliness?

✳ Can you think of some reasons why it would be good for you to go see them?

THEY'Ve BEEN THere

You will find that most Christians have been deeply lonely at one time or another. They will be able to sympathize with you and give added counsel that could send you down the road of fulfillment.

III. *THE THIRD STEP TO TAKE ABOUT LONELINESS IS TO REALIZE THAT GOD WANTS YOU TO SEEK THE FRIENDSHIP AND EMOTIONAL SUPPORT OF OTHERS.*

IT IS EASY IN OUR SOCIETY...

...which is socially disintegrated and mobile to pride ourselves on being a loner. We want to think we are able to take care of ourselves without the help of others. Deep down, we are protecting our own emotions while disobeying God's plan for us and doing some damage to our deepest needs. God's plan for us is to be in need of other people for fulfillment and growth.

Jesus clearly taught how important relationships with others are:

Matthew 22:35-39
(35)"And one of them, a lawyer, asked Him a question, testing Him,
(36)'Teacher, which is the great commandment in the Law?' And He said to
(37)him, ' "You shall love the Lord your God with all your heart, and
(38)with all your soul, and with all your mind.' This is the great and
(39)foremost commandment. And a second is like it, 'You shall
love your neighbor as yourself.'"

✳ *According to verse 39, what is the second most important thing you can do in life?* _____

✳ *Why is loving your neighbor so important?* _____

_____

OUR GREAT EXAMPLE FOR RELATIONSHIPS!

Jesus Christ is both uniquely God and man (the perfect God-man), and in His most crucial hour He deeply needed both communion with the Father, and with His closest friends.

Matthew 26:36-40
(36)"Then Jesus came with them to a place called Gethsemane, and said to
His disciples, 'Sit here while I go over there and pray.' And He
(37)took with Him Peter and the two sons of Zebedee, and began to be
(38)grieved and distressed. Then He said to them, 'My soul is deeply
grieved, to the point of death; remain here and keep watch with Me.'
(39)And He went a little beyond them, and fell on His face and prayed,
saying, 'My Father, if it is possible, let this cup pass from Me;
(40)yet not as I will, but as Thou wilt.' And He came to the disciples
and found them sleeping, and said to Peter, 'So, you men could not
keep watch with Me for one hour?'"

71

＊ In His deepest hour of agony, who(besides the Father) did Christ depend on? _____

＊ According to verse 38, was Christ afraid to show His deepest feelings?

_____

＊ According to verse 40, how important did He esteem His friend's support?

_____

> ## He NEEDED OTHERS
>
> *Jesus Christ is a clear example to us, for He trusted the Father with all His heart and yet, on the human level, felt the need to deeply relate and depend on His friends.*

IV. ANOTHER IMPORTANT STEP OUT OF YOUR LONELINESS IS TO COME TO LOVE AND UNDERSTAND THE VERY PRESENCE OF GOD IN YOUR DAILY LIFE.

> ## DOES HAVING More FRieNDS = LeSS LONeLiNeSS?
>
> *Most people feel that their loneliness problems would be solved if only they had more people around them to take away the gnaw of inner emptiness. What they fail to real-ize is that <u>unless they practice and understand God's "forever presence" in their innermost being, they will still remain deeply frustrated and lonely.</u>*

＊ What do you think is the difference between being alone and being lonely?

_____

JeSuS CHRiST SHoWeD uS...

...by His example, the differences between these when He was alone without loneliness:

John 6:15
"Jesus therefore perceiving that they were intending to come and take Him by force, to make Him king, withdrew again to the mountain by Himself alone."

✻ *In what condition did Jesus find Himself when He withdrew from the mountain?* _____

✻ *Do you think He was depressed while there, because He was not with the crowd?* _____

_____

JESUS WAS OFTEN IN SITUATIONS ALONE...

...but up until one particular moment on the cross, He was never lonely:

John 8:29
"And He who sent Me is with Me; He has not left Me alone, for I always do the things that are pleasing to Him."

✻ *Why, according to this verse, was Jesus not lonely?* _____

_____

HERE ARE SEVERAL LIFE SITUATIONS...

...where you may be left alone, but do not have to be lonely:

- *moving to a new location*

- *having no date on a Friday night*

- *socially isolated because of your stand for Christ*
  - ✻ *at work*
  - ✻ *at school*
  - ✻ *on an athletic team*
  - ✻ *at home*

JESUS WILL NEVER RIP US OFF!!

We need to practice the continued presence of God because, unlike our other friends, Jesus Christ never leaves us. Jesus said in Matthew 28:20, "And lo, I am with you always (those who are truly His), even to the end of the age." Again, the Bible says in Hebrews 13:5, "I will never desert you (His children), nor will I ever forsake you."

✳ How does one come to love and understand the presence of God?

_____

Lamentations 3:22-23
(22)"The Lord's lovingkindnesses indeed never cease, for His compassions
(23)never fail. They are new every morning; Great is Thy faithfulness."

✳ How can we experience His continued presence? _____

Psalm 63:1
"O God, Thou art my God; I shall seek Thee earnestly; My soul
thirsts for Thee, my flesh yearns for Thee, In a dry and weary land
where there is no water."

✳ According to this verse, what was David's life situation? _____

_____

✳ But Whom did David seek about this situation? _____

✳ According to the verse, did David have an impersonal God? _____


```
EVEN CLOSER THAN MOM OR DAD...
David was confident in God even though he was often
shunned by people, for he knew he had a Friend
Who lived within him.  That is why he wrote in Psalm
27:10, "For my father and my mother have forsaken me,
but the Lord will take me up."
```


IMPORTANT QUESTION:
✳ Can you think of ways to develop a closer friendship with God?
He wants to be your closest friend--the One Who meets your
deepest needs!

V. *THE NEXT STEP OUT OF LONELINESS IS TO FORGET OURSELVES AND TO REACH OUT IN A GIVING WAY TO OTHERS.*

There is no easy way out of loneliness. Overcoming isolation involves a process that will take place as we become a hard-working servant to others. As we serve those around us with great perserverance, an attitude will develop. It is the attitude of mutual commitment, which results in ongoing friendships that will greatly contribute to permanent relief from persisting loneliness.

ANoTHer WORD FoR LoNeLiNe$$

A person caught in loneliness can be caught in some of the most miserable <u>self-centeredness</u> that exists. The reason is because this person sees everything from <u>his own</u> needs and perspectives. That is why, if you have been lonely, you may have caught yourself saying things like:

✱ "Why doesn't anyone pay any attention to me?"

✱ "The other day, _____ ignored me."

✱ "There are so many cliques in the group, I can't possibly break into it."

✱ "The other day I heard _____ say something about me that hurt my feelings."

✱ "Why doesn't anyone care about me?"

The problem with all of these statements is the "I and me" complex. Such a person has become ingrown <u>rather than developing concern for others</u>.

The THREE ATTITUDES OF RELATING TO OTHERS THAT LEAD TO LASTING FRIENDSHIPS AND UNDERSTANDING.

A. *The first attitude is a responsible attitude.* Most everyone wants his freedom, but *many people are afraid to make permanent commitments* toward caring about someone else, for fear that this real concern would involve them in time, strain, sharing, and giving. They make temporary and superficial relationships, *yet they themselves need a much deeper level* of relationship to be happy.

Romans 15:1
"Now we who are strong ought to bear the weaknesses of those without strength *and not just please ourselves*."

✳ What is the responsibility of the strong? _____

_____

✳ Can you think of someone who may be weaker than you, and needs your help?

✳ According to the above verse, what are we doing if we are ignoring this responsibility? _____

THE COST

If we really want to reach out to others, we must realize that it will cost us involvement in their lives.

B. The second attitude you need is *the attitude of a servant.*

Matthew 20:26-28
(26) "It is not so among you, but whoever wishes to become great among you shall be your servant, and
(27) whoever wishes to be first among you shall be your slave; just as
(28) the Son of Man did not come to be served, but to serve, and to give His life a ransom for many."

*. What is the job of a servant? _____

*. If you really want to be fulfilled, and be part of God's greatness, what must you become? _____

*. Describe the attitudes and actions of a servant. _____

_____

_____

A SERVANT

A servant is one who puts himself out totally for the benefit of another. His attitudes and actions are directed toward the goal of meeting the needs of the one he serves. We, as Christians, are to exert our entire supply of energy as we strive to love and serve those around us.

We should not direct our attention to, nor fear the response of, the one being served, but because God loves us and totally serves our needs in Christ, we are to continue to strive to meet the needs of others with a servant's spirit.

Many Christians are afraid to reach out to any others for fear they will be misunderstood, unwanted and rejected. What they fail to realize is that many others around them feel the same way about themselves. They also forget that they are servants who have given up their privilege to have any say over whether they are accepted or rejected. A servant simply gives himself to the lives of others, regardless of response.

C. The third attitude one must have is the attitude of hard work.

We live in a society that has caused people to be fearful of one another. While inside they are crying out, their outside "front" can be hard and cold. It may take hard work to reach out to people who are like that.

Philippians 2:3-4

(3)*"Do nothing from selfishness or empty conceit. but with humility of mind let each of you regard one another as more important than*
(4)*himself; do not merely look out for your own personal interests, but also for the interests of others."*

✱*According to verse 4, whose interests are we to look out for?*

_____

TAKING THE PAIN OUT OF SOMEONE'S COLD RESPONSE TO OUR FRIENDSHIP

Often, in our own agony, we fail to see that others are emotionally hurting as badly, if not worse, than we are. When they in some way or another reject us, we tend to have fear rather than pity or compassion for that person. We should say to ourselves, "That person is acting this way not because of me, but because he/she has a deep need. The deeper the need, the more I need to keep loving that person back to spiritual health." EMOTIONAL HURTS

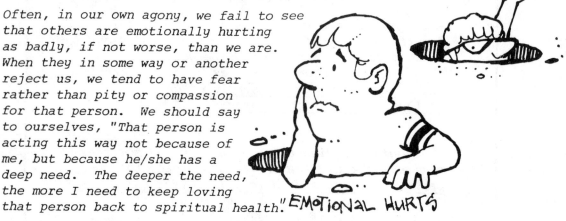

IMPORTANT QUESTION:

✱ *How enduring has Christ been to win our love for Him?* _____

_____

✱ *If Christ loved us in an outgoing way, how outgoing should we be in showing love to others?* _____

VI. *ONE WAY YOU CAN AVOID A LOT OF EMOTIONAL PAIN IS TO INTERPRET "THE ALONE TIMES" CORRECTLY.*

"GET IT ON!"

Ours is an action-oriented, noisy society. We get the idea from our culture that if we are not going somewhere actively and making a lot of noise about doing it, we are failing or something is wrong. Friday night may come, we have no date, there is silence in the house and we panic. We do need to use alone times to benefit ourselves and those we'll be serving later.

> Understand that being alone is not necessarily a sign of
> failure socially. (Jesus found times to be alone.)

Matthew 14:23
"And after He had sent the multitudes away, He went up to the mountain
by Himself to pray; and when it was evening, He was there alone."

Who had Jesus been with all day? _____

ENJOY BEING ALONE

During periods of our lives we often spend great
amounts of time with all kinds of people. We may
not know it, but in reality we are being emotionally, physically and sometimes spiritually drained.
God desires that we be alone, get quiet, and
re-assess our activity and our future. Don't let
the sudden quiet depress us; we should welcome it
as a friend. Jesus sought these times alone.

✳✳ Here are some practical things you can be doing in times alone:

1. THINK.

Take time to think through your life, and ponder the
things you've been doing. Your values, goals, friends,
and future can all be considered. In quietness you
may be able to get a calmer, clearer perspective of
your whole life. How often have you said to yourself,
"I just need to get alone and think"?

Isaiah 30:15b
"In repentance and rest you shall be saved, In quietness and trust
is your strength."

> Some of the richest times
> in your life can come from
> your quietly thinking alone.

2. PRAY.

While it is true that you need to grow in Christ through fellowship with other Christians, there are times to just get to know God by spending time with Him alone in prayer. Jesus did this.

3 READ YOUR BIBLE.

David, because of his position as king of Israel and his numerous, godless enemies, spent many hours alone. This is what he said about it:

Psalm 119:23-24

(23)"Even though princes sit and talk against me, Thy servant meditates
(24)on thy statutes. Thy testimonies also are my delight; They are my counselors."

✳ *According to verse 23, why did king David have seemingly good cause to be depressed while he was alone?* _____

✳ *In verse 24, why was it that he was so thrilled with what he read?*

_____

4. READ GOOD BOOKS.

The Bible tells us that the apostle Paul was in prison near the end of his life. He had every reason to be lonely, for he knew he was going to die soon. But this is what he asked for in a letter to his friend, Timothy:

II Timothy 4:13
"When you come bring the cloak which I left at Troas with Carpus, and the books, especially the parchments."

> Paul was asking for his books
> and the Scripture. Alone times
> are great for reading a book,
> and growing as a person by them.

CONCLUSION...

- *God is a loving Person Who does not want you to be frustrated by either being alone or lonely.*

- *God wants you to turn your loneliness into victory and your alone times into deep growing experiences.*

- *God wants you to be aware of the pain of hundreds of people around us so that we, as people who have been lonely, will be able to share Christ's love--which can end loneliness.*

AS YOU REACH OUT, CLAIM THESE VERSES ...

I Corinthians 1:3-4
"Grace to you and peace from God our Father and the Lord Jesus Christ. I thank my God always concerning you, for the grace of God which was given you in Christ Jesus."

NOTES

The importance of understanding
PARENTS
Discussion 5

RATE YOUR PARENTS ON THE SCALE BELOW..

* *Do you know why you have hassles with your parents?*

* *Are the conflicts in your relationship mostly your parents fault?*

* *Is the conflict mostly your fault?*

* *To what extent does your relationship with your parents affect your day?*

HAVE YOU REALIZED THAT YOUR RELATIONSHIP WITH YOUR PARENTS WILL GREATLY AFFECT MANY AREAS OF YOUR LIFE?

It will affect the way you view...

> ●*yourself*
> ●*your date life*
> ●*your studies*
> ●*your future marriage*
> ●*your relationships with your friends*
> ●*your future*
> ●*your walk with God*
> ●*your peace of mind*

✳ *Do you know why the relationship you have with your parents greatly affects your walk with God?*

SOMETHING IN COMMON

God, your parents, your employer, your teachers, the government, and the police all have something in common as they relate to your life. They are all authority figures. God, of course, being the greatest authority and all other authority coming beneath Him have various degrees of effect upon your life.

WHAT IS AN AUTHORITY FIGURE?

An authority figure is any person God has placed over you who will be used by Him to accomplish His purpose in your life.

WHAT IS THE BIGGEST PROBLEM...

...we face as we deal with authority figures? <u>*It is pride.*</u>

PRIDE...

...shows itself in rebellion. Rebellion is an attitude which we have as a result of our sin nature. This attitude fights anyone who might tell us what to do or how to live. Nothing has so destructively effected man's existence as has his pride and rebellion. Consequently, when we allow a bad habit of rebellion toward authority figures to control us, it will cause deep conflict in our walk with God.

Romans 13:1-2
(1) *"Let every person be in subjection to the governing authorities. For there is no authority except from God, and those which exist*
(2) *are established by God. Therefore he who resists authority has opposed the ordinance of God; and they who have opposed will receive condemnation upon themselves."*

✳ *How closely linked is the authority figure to God?* _____

_____

✴ From verse 1, is there any person in authority over you whom God has not put there? _____

_____

✴ Is it logical to assume that God has put our parents over us? _____

_____

Since the relationship we have with our parents affects so many areas of our lives, and especially our walk with God, it would be wise to discuss God's method of living peacefully together.

LET'S DISCUSS WHAT STEP YOU CAN TAKE THAT WILL ASSURE YOU A SUCCESSFUL RELATIONSHIP WITH YOUR PARENTS...

I. _The first step to having a better relationship with your parents is for you to decide to be a peacemaker._

Matthew 5:9 (Living Bible)
"Happy are the peacemakers, for they shall be called sons of God."

Each of us has a great desire to be happy, but few are willing to pay the price to obtain that happiness. Jesus said that we would be happy if we would become peacemakers. However, being a peacemaker is no easy task. The question we need to ask ourselves is this: "How badly do we really desire to have peace with our family?" If we desire it enough, and are willing to trust God for it, then that peace is within our reach.

A. _There are three qualities which we must have in order to become_
peacemakers.

1. _You must primarily become aware of your parents' needs._
   It's easy to look for their faults, and to overemphasize
   how "awful" they are.   Your parents might actually be:

   • _too strict_
     • _too overprotective_
       • _too old-fashioned_
         • _not understanding_
           • _set in their ways_
             • _unrealistic_
               • _insensitive to your needs_
               • _too bossy_
                 • _and so on, and so on..._

God does not want us to focus our attention on their weaknesses as a
justification for our rebellion.

Matthew 7:3-5
"And why do you look at the speck that is in your brother's eye,
but do not notice the log that is in
your own eye?   Or how can you say to
your brother, 'Let me take the speck
out of your eye,' and behold the log
is in your own eye?   You hypocrite,
first take the log out of your own
eye, and then you will see clearly
to take the speck out of your
brother's eye."

It is simple for us to find
fault with our parents and to
dwell on the many ways they
could improve.   God desires
that we work on any shortcomings
we might have before we think
about helping our parents and
others to become like Christ.

THE FIRST STEP...

The first step to being a peacemaker, then, is to put away our hostile, judgmental attitude toward our parents and begin to view their needs and interests as a top priority in our lives.

2. <u>The second quality of a peacemaker is the willingness on our part to become vulnerable.</u>

✻ *What does it mean to be vulnerable?* _____

_____

God understands what it is to be vulnerable. He continually loves the world, day after day, even when it continues to reject Him.

To be a peacemaker you must get up time after time, even when you have been hurt. It means that you keep opening yourself up to your parents and it means remaining very vulnerable to them.

I Corinthians 13:5
(Love) does not take into account a wrong suffered."

✳ Have your parents ever wronged you?

✳ What was your reaction to that wrong?

✳ What are your feelings toward the incident right now?

✳ From verse 5, how does God tell us to handle wrong?

HeRe's The ATTiTuDe.

Because God continues to love and forgive us He desires for us to do the same for our parents and retain a servant's spirit and attitude.

---

3. The third quality of a peacemaker is that he is willing to face injustices.

There have been, or will be times when your parents will make accusations and decisions about you which are entirely wrong. The test of a peacemaker is in how he responds to the injustices others inflict upon him.

I Peter 2:18-20(Living Bible)
(18)"Servants, you must respect your masters and do whatever they tell you
   --not only if they are kind and reasonable, but even if they are tough
(19)and cruel. Praise the Lord if you are punished for doing right! Of
(20)course, you get no credit for being patient if you are beaten for doing
   wrong; but if you do right and suffer for it, and are patient beneath
   the blows, God is well pleased."

✳According to verse 18, are we to be respectful to only those
   authority figures who are good and loving? _____

✱ According to verse 20, what attitude should we have when we are wronged?

_____

_____

✱ According to verse 20, what is God's response to our patience as we face injustice? _____

_____

If your parents are not Christians, you may suffer great misunderstanding and persecution right within your own home.

Matthew 10:34-36
(34)"Do not think that I cam to bring peace on the earth; I did not come
(35)to bring peace, but a sword. For I came to set a man against his
     father, and a daughter against her mother, and a daughter-in-law
(36)against her mother-in-law; and a man's enemies will be members of
     his household."

DON'T BE SURPRISED!

God does not want you to be surprised when you are treated unjustly. He wants you to look after your parents' needs, be vulnerable to them, and be ready at times to be treated unfairly. He just wants us to love them in His power. If you will trust Him in this area, you are on your way to becoming happy.

A WORD OF CAUTION...

It is possible that you will be greatly misunderstood within your family because of your faith in Christ. Do not use this as a reason for not loving and obeying them. The Bible tells us, "When a man's ways are pleasing to the Lord, He makes even his enemies to be at peace with him." (Proverbs 16:7)

II. Not only must you be a peacemaker in your home to be happy, but the second step to real happiness with your parents comes when you learn to obey them.

Ephesians 6:1-3(Living Bible)
(1)"Children, obey your parents; this is the right thing to do because
(2)God has placed them in authority over you. Honor your mother and
     father. This is the first of God's Ten Commandments that ends with
(3)a promise. And this is the promise: that if you honor your mother
     and father, yours will be a long life, full of blessing."

✱ According to verse 1, why should we obey our parents? _____

_____

✳ *According to verse 3, what are the benefits of obeying our parents?*

¡MPORTANT!

·*It is important to see that God has given our parents certain acquired abilities that will help us obtain qualities in our lives that He desires us to have.*

A. <u>The first ability our parents have is to see events, people and circumstances that will do us great harm.</u>

1. *Our parents have already experienced many of the situations that we will encounter in the future. They have made mistakes and learned lessons that we could benefit by, if we would give attention to their advice. They have tremendous insights that are valuable to us concerning:*

✳ *jobs*   ✳ *dating*

✳ *friends*   ✳ *finances*

✳ *education* ✳ *personal responsibilities*

" IT SEEMS TO ME "

Often when parents say, "I have learned..." or, "It seems to me..." --they are speaking from their own experience. It is wise to listen to their instruction, for they may have already gone through what we are facing.

2. *In Proverbs 5, a father gives his son instruction concerning types of people with whom he should not associate. In verses 12-14 of the same chapter, the father warns his son of what he will say to himself if he fails to heed important fatherly counsel.*

Proverbs 5:12-14(Living Bible)
(12)"and you say, 'Oh, if only I had listened!
If only I had not demanded my own way!
Oh, why wouldn't I take advice? Why was I so stupid?
For now I must face public disgrace."

3. God desires us to be wise, not thinking that we have all the answers. As we know, we do not have all the answers, so it is important to listen and obey the instruction of our parents.

Proverbs 12:15
"The way of a fool is right in his own eyes, But a wise man is he who listens to counsel."

B Another acquired ability our parents have is to discern certain rough edges in our attitudes which could be detrimental to us the rest of our lives. They not only can discern these rough edges, but also have the ability to become "sand paper" to smooth the rough edges off our lives.

God has designed life...

...so that our parents know something about our personality and the way we think. Our parents have lived with most of us for quite awhile. They can see strengths and weaknesses in us that we might not see.

When parents discipline us...

...they are probably aware of some attitude which might hurt us for the rest of our lives if it isn't dealt with. These attitudes are the same areas that God desires us to change.

Some of these attitudes:

✳ _Laziness_--few people who have an attitude like this are ever very successful at anything in life for very long.

✳ _Ungratefulness_--usually people do not like to be around those who take others for granted.

✳ _Temper_--it is not wise or even safe to be around people who lose their temper; in fact, God warns against it.

✳ _Pride_--do you like to be around people who think they are better than you?

✳ _Rudeness_--have you ever realized how most rude people are left standing alone?

✳ _Selfishness_--have you ever noticed how selfish people are unhappy people?

❋ _Sloppiness_--most people who are sloppy waste time by trying to get organized.

❋ _Unforgiving spirit_--there are many people living lives of hostility and bitterness because they have never learned to forgive.

IT IS ABSOLUTELY CRUCIAL...

...to know that God is using our parents to weed out bad attitudes. If we do not co-operate with God and our folks, He simply finds another author-ity figure (teacher, employer, government official, police, warden) to keep working on us. The problem is that each time some new author-ity figure has to become sand paper to smooth the rough edges of our per-sonality, it becomes all the more painful for us. Cooperate with God by obey-ing your parents as they love, instruct and discipline you now.

Proverbs 15:31-32(Living Bible)
(31)"If you profit from constructive criticism you will be elected to the
(32)wise men's hall of fame. But to reject criticism is to harm yourself and your own best interests."

REMEMBER:

When you take discipline from your parents, you are really taking it from the Lord. And, remember that what you are taking is a form of love!

Proverbs 3:11-12(Living Bible)
"Young man, do not resent it when God chastens and corrects you, for His punishment is proof of His love. Just as a father punishes a son he delights in to make him better, so the Lord corrects you."

C. Here are some practical steps to take which will contribute to a better relationship with your parents. _Ask yourself some difficult questions, and seek to be honest:_

❋ Have I in any way done something that has hurt my parents?

✳ *Am I really cooperating with God as He strives to work through my parents to smooth out some rough spots in my life?*

Step ONE: SEEK YOUR PARENT'S FORGIVENESS
If you have wronged your parents, you no doubt have hurt their feelings and deeply offended them. Sit down and have a talk with them. Look them straight in the eye and ask them if they will forgive you for the bad attitudes you have had and the grief you have given them. Make sure you obtain their forgiveness before leaving.

Step Two: COOPERATE WITH YOUR PARENTS
Ask them to share with you the attitudes you portray that they don't like. As you submit these bad attitudes to God and allow Him to change them, you will see your parents change as well.

Step THRee: TELL YOUR PARENTS YOU LOVE THEM
It may take great courage to show love for your parents, but it's worth it. Your parents may have been waiting a long time to hear those meaningful words, "I love you!"

Step FoUR: THANK YOUR PARENTS FOR ALL THAT THEY HAVE DONE FOR YOU
Most parents have a good memory about all the things they have done for you. They no doubt think that the sacrifice was worth it, but they probably would appreciate a little recognition.

Step FiVe: AVOID RAISING YOUR VOICE WITH YOUR PARENTS ANYTIME
One sure way to start a real argument with misunderstandings and hurt feelings is to raise your voice during a discussion. Even if your parents are yelling at the top of their lungs, keep your voice down; that will really help.

(Proverbs 15:1 - "A gentle answer turns away wrath...")

Step SiX: LET GOD CHANGE YOUR PARENT'S MINDS; THAT'S HIS JOB, NOT YOURS
It is often difficult when your parents refuse to give you permission to do something you really want to do. Take their answer as coming from God, and go to him in prayer about the situation. As you know, God is very powerful, and He can work to change your parent's mind any time He wills it.

(Proverbs 21:1 - "Just as water is turned into irrigation ditches, so the Lord directs the king's thoughts. He turns them wherever He wants to.") (Living Bible)

STeP SeVeN: *ASTOUND YOUR PARENTS BY THE OVER-OBEDIENT METHOD*

Let's say you ask your parents if you can go with some friends somewhere on a Friday night. They refuse to give you permission and, instead, tell you to do a job like wash the car or clean out the garage or do the dishes. Your parents have reasoned out that you are not quite mature enough yet for the Friday night adventure. They have a chore that you can do that will give you more maturity. The worst thing you can do is to get upset and cause a scene. When you get upset, you only <u>reinforce</u> in your parent's minds that which they are already thinking; that you are too immature to handle this situation. Use an opportunity such as this one just described to try the OVER-OBEDIENT method. The next time they say "no" to you and then give you a job to do, make sure you not only do the job they ask for, but do one task they didn't ask you to do. If your mother asks you to do the dishes--don't <u>just</u> do the dishes but maybe clean the living room (or some other project) as well. Then go to your mother and say, "I've done the dishes and have cleaned the living room; is there anything else you want me to do? Not only will this blow your parents minds but, after a few attempts at this method (done sincerely by you), you will begin to see it pay off...

PRaCTiCe THiS VerSe:

Proverbs 25:15 (Living Bible)
"Be patient and you finally win, for a soft tongue can break hard bones."

III. <u>The final step you can take in having a happy home is to see life from your parent's point of view.</u>

At times, our parents act and say things in a way that totally baffles us. It is easy at those times to get upset and shut them out of our lives. Rather than alienating them during these times of pressure, we should ask ourselves, "What emotional pressures are they facing that cause them to act the way they do?" Consider these pressures that may be affecting your parent's relationship with you:

PaReNT'S PoiNT of VieW

LIFE LIFE

FaTHeR:
- *is he facing problems at work?*
- *does he feel fulfilled in his life?*
- *is he experiencing a time of loneliness?*
- *is he bored?*
- *has anyone deeply hurt him lately?*
- *are he and mom getting along?*
- *is his sex life together?*

MOTHER:

- *does she feel like people really appreciate her?*
- *is she under financial pressure?*
- *is it hard for her to work and be a mother at the same time?*
- *does she sense that she isn't needed?*
- *does she become upset because she's insecure?*
- *is she facing change of life?*
- *is her sex life fulfilling?*
- *is dad giving her enough attention?*

THEY NEED YOU!

Your parents could be in great emotional pain and you may not even be aware of it. When they are facing deep emotional pressures, the last thing they need is to be hassled by you. But, they need your understanding, and they need you!

I John 3:18 (Living Bible)
"Little children, let us stop just saying we love people; let us really love them, and show it by our actions."

YOUR FATHER...

...needs to know that you respect and value his counsel. Can you think of some questions that would enable him to share some of his thoughts and opinions concerning your:

* *school*
* *work*
* *friends*
* *future*
* *mother (his wife)*
* *role in his dreams*

(TIP: When you ask these questions of him, don't argue, just listen.)

...desires respect and attention. Could you compliment and thank her concerning some of these things:

* *cooking meals*
* *washing your clothes*
* *keeping the house clean*
* *her appearance*

- *Are there places you can take her for an evening to show your appreciation?*

* *shopping*
* *out to dinner*
* *fashion show*
* *tennis*

We have discussed three steps...

...you can take in order to establish a happier and more fulfilling relationship with your parents. The first was to <u>decide to become a peacemaker;</u> the second was <u>learning to obey them;</u> and the third was <u>trying to see life from their perspective.</u>

*Is there ever a time when you should disobey your parents? _____

_____

Acts 5:28-29
"'We give you strict orders to continue teaching in this name, and behold you have filled Jerusalem with your teaching and intend to bring this man's blood upon us!" But Peter and the Apostles answered and said, 'We must obey God rather than men.'"

A word of caution!

If you really trust, obey and follow God's counsel concerning your relationship with your parents, then there will probably never be a time when you will have to disobey them.

If you truly desire peace, Christ will change any problems in your family to bring about His peace and harmony!

NOTES

The importance of understanding
SEX
DiSCUSSiON 6

THE POWER OF SEX.

If you live in the youth culture of today or have recently passed through it, you have no doubt struggled with the drives, the joys, and the hassles of sex. Sex impulses, sex thoughts and sex actions seem to be the most puzzling factors in the lives of youth. Confusion and emotional pain result when a person has an improper understanding of the intimate, powerful reality of sex.

ANSWERING THESE QUESTIONS...

...will help you to discern your attitude and views about sex:

✳ *Do you believe that sex is "dirty" and that it should only be used for the purpose of having children?*

✳ *Do you think sex before marriage is justifiable because:*

* *it helps you understand how you really feel about the person you are dating*
* *the two of you plan on marriage soon anyway*
* *it will teach you how to be a "better lover" in marriage*
* *this intimate method will help you find out whether you're compatible*

✳ *Do you think that sex before marriage is wrong? Why?*

✳ *How far do you think you can go on a date?*

✳ *Do you think that fantasizing (day dreaming) about sex is a healthy emotional habit?*

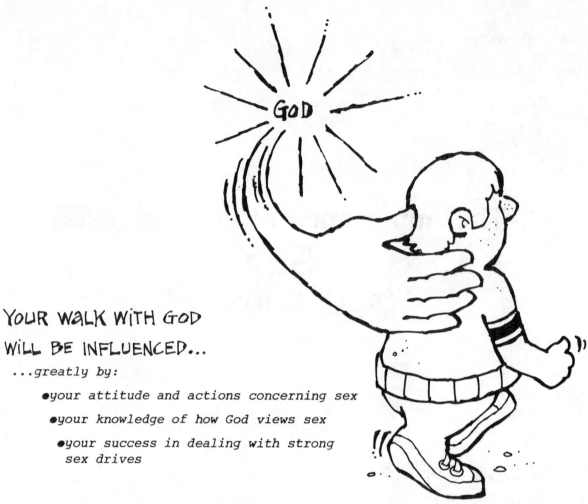

YOUR WALK WITH GOD
WILL BE INFLUENCED...

...*greatly by:*

- *your attitude and actions concerning sex*
- *your knowledge of how God views sex*
- *your success in dealing with strong sex drives*

LET'S CONSIDER THE TOPIC OF SEX...

...*as far as the way God views sex, and the way we can practically respond to God's instruction, that we might have a fulfilled sex life.*

I. *Why does sex have such a great influence upon your life?*

A.. *SEX DRIVES*

If you are a male and between the ages of 16 and 25, or female and in your late 20's or early 30's, then the strongest drive you are probably experiencing is your sex drive. This is not to say that a man's sex drive ends at 25 years old, or that a woman's begins at 25; it is simply an indicator that the sex drives are often at their strongest during this time.

"SEX" ISN'T EQUAL TO "SIN"

You need to know that sex drives (impulses) are not sin. Accept the fact that you have these, and that God has given them to you.

B. EMOTIONAL AND SECURITY DRIVES

When two people of opposite sexes have interaction (defined here as activity ranging from holding hands to having sexual relations) they are usually looking for more than just sexual stimulation, and there is often a desire to give and accept love, support, and emotional security.

✳ Where does the problem concerning sex begin? _____

_____

IT'S NORMAL To HaVE DEEP NEEDS

Don't become upset with yourself for having deep needs--the desire to be loved and to show deep affection to someone else--but realize that you have the elements of an explosive situation when your emotional needs and your sex drive meet.

C. OUR SOCIETY IS SEX CRAZY

✳ Have you heard any songs on the radio that allude to sex and intimate sexual activity?

✳ Do you remember seeing a movie when there was no sexual activity at all?

✳ Have you noticed the increase of sexual activity on TV?

✳ Are you aware of the advertiser's attempts to manipulate your sex drives and to get you to buy their products?

✳ Have you noticed an emphasis upon sex when some of these products are advertised on TV, on billboards, and in magazines?

- shaving cream - cigarettes - toothpaste - cars
- hair coloring - suntan lotion
  - liquor
  - clothing
  - milk
  - nylons
  - airlines
  - restaurants
  - movie ads
  - real estate
  - "you-name-it"

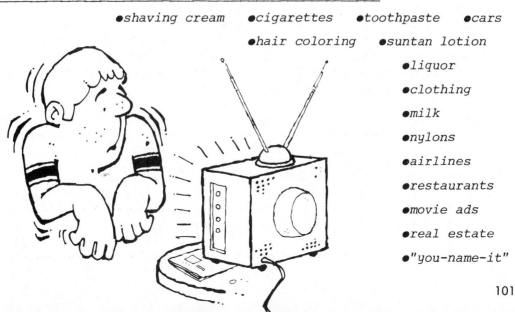

II. How does God view sex?

A. SINCE GOD IS THE CREATOR OF SEX...

...it is His desire that it be enjoyed and appreciated to its best and fullest potential. According to God's Word, this can only occur within a marriage relationship.

GOD DESIGNED MAN WITH SEX POTENTIAL...

...and from God's perspective, sex is a good thing--a real blessing! He desires that those whom He calls into marriage have full sexual fulfillment as He designed it.

Genesis 1:27,28,31
(27)"And God created man in His own image, in the image of God He created
(28)him; male and female He created them. And God blessed them; and God said to them, 'Be fruitful and multiply, and fill the earth'... And
(31)God saw all that He had made and behold it was very good..."

* According to verse 28, God says, "Be fruitful and multiply and fill the earth." Do you think it is possible to be fruitful and multiply and fill the earth without having sex? _____ No _____

* What was God's attitude as He viewed His design for sex? _____

_____

B. JESUS CHRIST APPROVED OF SEX

...between a husband and his wife.

Matthew 19:4-6
"And He answered and said, "Have you not read, that He who created them from the beginning MADE THEM MALE AND FEMALE, and said, "FOR THIS CAUSE A MAN SHALL LEAVE HIS FATHER AND MOTHER, AND SHALL CLEAVE TO HIS WIFE; AND THE TWO SHALL BECOME ONE FLESH"? Consequently they are no more two, but one flesh. What therefore God has joined together, let no man separate."

* What did Jesus mean when He said the two shall become one flesh? _____

_____

C. IT IS GOD'S DESIRE THAT GREAT ENJOYMENT COME FROM SEX...

...and from a sexual relationship within marriage. While sexual intercourse in marriage is a truly holy event, God also intended it to be pleasurable(downright fun!).

Proverbs 5:18,19
"Let your fountain be blessed, And rejoice in the wife of your youth. As a loving hind and a graceful doe, Let her breasts satisfy you at all times; Be exhilarated always with her love."

(God intends for married people, united in Him, to deeply enjoy each other's bodies. He has designed the human body for his glory, but has also tailored it for the enjoyment of the marriage partners. God's goal for married couples is to explore and derive pleasure from each other's love and physical make-up. This means that a husband is to be satisfied by the physical relationship he has with his own wife.)

I Corinthians 7:2-5 (Living Bible)
"But usually it is best to be married, each man having his own wife, and each woman having her own husband, because otherwise you might fall back into sin. The man should give his wife all that is her right as a married woman, and the wife should do the same for her husband: for a girl who marries no longer has full right to her own body, for her husband then has his rights to it, too; and in the same way the husband no longer has full right to his own body, for it belongs also to his wife. So do not refuse these rights to each other. The only exception to this rule would be the agreement of both husband and wife to refrain from the rights of marriage for a limited time, so that they can give themselves more completely to prayer. Afterwards, they should come together again so that Satan won't be able to tempt them because of their lack of self-control."

SEX AND THE BIBLE

The Bible makes it very clear that God wants Christians to have the most vibrant, exciting sex life possible. Since this is true He gives us the following instructions.

III. *God is clearly in favor of sex within marriage, but He is flatly and openly against involved loveplay before marriage.*

A. *GOD'S VIEW IS SHOWN CLEARLY IN:*

I Thessalonians 4:3-5 (Living Bible)
"For God wants you to be holy, and pure, and to keep clear of all sexual sin, so that each of you will marry in holiness and honor--not in lustful passion as the heathen do, in their ignorance of God and His ways."

✳ *According to verse 5, what is God's will for us as we face involvement in sexual sin?* _____

✳ *What is sexual sin?* _____

✳ What condition does God want us to be in when we marry? _____

_____

✳ What happens when we do not keep clear of sexual sin? _____

_____

DO YOU WANT GOD DISPLEASED ?

God tells us that it is against His will for us to have premarital sex. He also clearly states that we are to completely stay away from any activity that relates to the misuse of sex.

Ephesians 5:3-4(Living Bible)
"Let there be no sex sin, impurity or greed among you. Let no one be able to accuse you of such things. Dirty stories, foul talk and coarse jokes--these are not for you. Instead, remind each other of God's goodness and be thankful."

✳ According to verse 3, does God tolerate any degree of sex sin? _____

✳ According to verse 4, what are the other activities related to the misuse of sex? _____

IS GOD THE GREAT "KILL-JOY" CONCERNING SEX ?

HARDLY...

Why does God put restr ctions on heavy loveplay and sex before marriage? Is it because He doesn't want us to enjoy ourselves? Hardly! God gives us His loving counsel and command so that we might enjoy sex more, not less.

IV. *Here are five reasons why God has given us His loving commands about sex:*

A. *GOD WANTS US TO SEEK AND EXPERIENCE THE TRUE MEANING OF LOVE.*

1. *Jesus clearly stated that His primary concern for our lives was that we learn to love God and others.*

Matthew 22:37-40
"And He said to him, 'You shall love the Lord your God will all your heart, and with all your soul, and with all your mind.' This is the great and foremost commandment. The second is like it, 'You shall love your neighbor as yourself.' On these two commandments depend the whole Law and the Prophets."

2. *Paul instructs us concerning what real love is.*

I Corinthians 13:1-3
"If I speak with the tongues of men and of angels, but do not have love, I have become a noisy gong or a clanging cymbal. And if I have the gift of prophecy, and know all mysteries and all knowledge; and if I have all faith, so as to remove mountains, but do not have love, I am nothing. And if I give all my possessions to feed the poor, and if I deliver my body to be burned, but do not have love, it profits me nothing."

THE POINT TO REALIZE IS THAT LOVE IS NOT SEX, AND SEX IS NOT LOVE!

WHAT SEX IS NOT:
God wants us to know that sex in and of itself is not love. Without real love, sex is nothing more than a self-centered desire for sensual pleasure. Nowhere in the Bible will you find that sex is defined as love. A person can experience great disillusionment and sorrow if he feels he can find love by sex alone. Even though sex can be emotionally explosive, it is not love.

> ## WHaT SEX iS:
> God has designed sex as a physical expression of love
> between a husband and his wife. While love will grow
> without sex, sex without love becomes a destructive
> exercise and an exploitation of the other person.

3. <u>The difference between love and sex:</u>

Many people confuse sex with love.
They often allow sex to act as a
counterfeit for real love.
Here are a list of differences
between real love and sex.

"Love"	"SEX-FOR-SEX'S-SaKE"
<u>Love</u> must have respect to grow.	Sex-for-sex's-sake does not demand respect in the other person; in fact, it may cause lack of respect to grow and flourish. (Everyone wants respect.)
<u>Love</u>, in order to grow, takes continual attention and hard work.	<u>Sex</u>, in and of itself, takes little hard work and needs only a limited amount of attention temporarily.
<u>Love</u> is an act of the will that continues on in spite of little or negative feelings. Love will continue by an act of the will even if a person doesn't feel like it.	<u>Sex</u> is an act of the will that is dependent upon feelings. It is because of deeply aroused feelings, or supposed feelings of pleasure and intimacy, that one gets involved in sexual activity.
<u>Love</u> takes a long time to grow and therefore takes patience and endurance for its maturity.	<u>Sex</u> can happen very quickly and needs very little time to evolve.
<u>Love</u> requires meaningful communication and thoughtful interaction between two people.	<u>Sex</u> does not demand that you verbally share with your partner.
<u>Love</u> is an art that is learned from others and from the power of God. It involves many little actions that lead to a meaningful existence.	<u>Sex</u> is not a learned art, but is known by natural instincts, and is one big action that brings about a comprehensive feeling.

IT IS BECAUSE OF THESE THINGS THAT GOD CLEARLY STATES:

Philippians 1:9 (Living Bible)
"My prayer for you is that you will overflow more and more with love for others, and at the same time keep growing in spiritual knowledge and insight."

Colossians 3:5 (Living Bible)
Away then with sinful, earthly things; deaden the evil desires lurking within you; have nothing to do with sexual sin, impurity, lust and shameful desires; don't worship the good things in life, for that is idolatry."

God wants us to understand the importance of focusing our time and effort in a dating relationship on the non-physical activities.

Those qualities which hold your relationship together need much time and consideration before they can develop. Some of these qualities are:

✱ *trust*

  ✱ *respect*

    ✱ *open communication*

      ✱ *honest spiritual communication*

        ✱ *deep friendship*

If you take your eyes off of these elements and focus on the physical, your relationship will self-destruct.

B. GOD GIVES HIS LOVING COMMANDS CONCERNING SEX TO PROTECT US ALL FROM THE HARMFUL PSYCHOLOGICAL AND PHYSICAL EFFECTS OF ITS MISUSE.

HE NEVER INTENDED...
God never intended man to bed-hop from person to person. His goal for sex has always been within the boundaries of marriage.

Proverbs 4:15-20 (Living Bible)
"Avoid their haunts--turn away, go somewhere else, for evil men don't sleep until they've done their evil deed for the day. They can't rest unless they cause someone to stumble and fall. They eat and drink wickedness and violence!

Proverbs 4:15-20 (continued)
"But the good man walks along in the ever-brightening light of God's favor; the dawn gives way to morning splendor, while the evil man gropes and stumbles in the dark. Listen, son of mine, to what I say. Listen carefully."

Watch out Fella!

Since sex is such an intimate, highly emotional event, it has deep psychological effects on its participants. It has the potential of causing one to feel more involved with the other than could ever be imagined. <u>*To misuse sex can cause emotional conflict and damage which is not easily straightened out, and may never be--apart from the grace of God!*</u>

Three Harmful Psychological Effects of the misuse of sex are:

1. Unfulfilled emotional needs that tend to lead to frustration and bitterness.

2. The potential that crippling emotional habits could likely develop.

3. A disappointment resulting from the use of sex to fulfill the need for love.

(see chart on next page)

108

HERE are THREE PSYCHOLOGICAL "COME-DOWNS" THAT CAN RESULT FROM THE MISUSE OF SEX

SEX IS:	SEX CAN CAUSE:	RESULT OF THE MISUSE OF SEX:
1. Sex is an intimate act. If sex is used apart from love, it can cause people to feel a false sense of closeness.	1. Sex can cause a deep desire to: ●spend many hours with the other person ●have the other person accept you just as you are ●be understood by the other person ●be needed by the other person	1. Sex can cause emotional desires but cannot lastingly fulfill them. If sex is used as a game—just to satisfy physical desires—it will stir up needs which only true love can satisfy. Therefore, one or both of the partners could possibly create a deeper need in the other than he or she is either willing or capable of fulfilling. A partner whose needs have been aroused but not met is very susceptible to becoming bitter and hostile.
2. Sex is designed by God to bring great pleasure to the marriage partners. It is an enjoyable experience which can frequently be partaken of.	2. Sex can cause: ●pleasure temporarily ●a habit, if one becomes involved in it again and again.	2. The person who is hooked on the misuse of sex can be addicted to an act which gives temporary pleasure, but longer-lasting emotional pain. It is possible to become a slave to one's own glands! I Corinthians 6:12-13 "All things are lawful for me, but not all things are profitable. All things are lawful for me, but I will not be mastered by anything. Food is for the stomach, and the stomach is for food; but God will do away with both of them. Yet the body is not for immorality, but for the Lord; and the Lord is for the body."
3. Sex is an exciting and mean-ingful event that most people look forward to from their early teens. Sex is—without a loving relationship (as evidenced by a commitment of responsibility in marriage)—a fleeting pleasure which tends to end in emptiness and loss.	3. Sex can cause: ●thoughts of pleasure CHECK OUT: Proverbs 14:13 Proverbs 4:19	3. A problem occurs when a person begins to experiment with sex, hoping to find a satisfying experience without first having the prerequisite of love which would make it fulfilling. A common result of this experimenting is disillusionment and disappointment. A person will often be deceived into thinking that learning different sex techniques will bring back the pleasure and fulfillment he seeks. This type of involvement always ends in boredom.

C. THE THIRD REASON GOD GIVES US HIS LOVING COMMAND ABOUT SEX IS THAT HE WANTS TO PROTECT OUR FUTURE MARRIAGE.

1. <u>God views marriage as a life-long commitment.</u>

Matthew 19:4-9 (Living Bible)
"'Don't you read the Scriptures?' He replied. 'In them it is written
(5) that at the beginning God created man and woman, and that a man should
(6) leave his father and mother and be forever united to his wife. The two
shall become one --no longer two, but one! And no man may divorce
(7) what God has joined together.' 'Then why,' they asked, 'did Moses say
a man may divorce his wife by merely writing her a letter of dismissal?'
(8) Jesus replied, 'Moses did that in recognition of your hard and evil
hearts, but it was not what God had originally intended. And I tell
(9) you this, that anyone who divorces his wife, except for fornication,
and marries another, commits adultery.'"

✳ According to verse 6, what degree of solidarity did Jesus say the marriage relationship was to have? _____

✳ According to verse 9, what are the only grounds for divorce? _____

2. ANSWer THESE QUESTIONS ...
...to help clarify how you feel about marriage.

✳ Would you like to have a successful marriage?

✳ Would you mind your husband or wife having sex with other people?

✳ To what degree do you think trust and respect will influence your marriage?

✳ When you and your partner are separated, how do you know he or she is not having sex with someone else?

3. A key to having a successful future marriage is to develop the attributes of self-control within your life now.

a. If one or both of the marriage partners have not developed habits of self-control while they were young, there is a great possibility that there will be extramarital sexual activity when they are married.

b. A person who has formed a pattern of poor self-control before marriage (by being involved in premarital sexual activity) could possibly be difficult to respect and trust.

c. If your marriage partner had very little self-control before marriage, what makes you feel that he will be content and satisfied with you for an entire lifetime? For example: maybe you'll be sick, or too tired, or pregnant, or not in the mood for sex. Without the quality of self-control, why do you feel your partner will be faithful?

d. As we can see, developing the quality of self-control early in life is very important. It is something necessary to have even during your dating years. God clearly warns against trying to face life without the quality of self-control.

Proverbs 25:28
"Like a city that is broken into and without walls is a man who has no control over his spirit."

    e. The key to the development of self-control in your life is in allowing the power of the Holy Spirit the freedom to permeate every area of your life.

Galatians 5:22-23
"But the fruit of the Spirit is love, joy, peace, patience, kindness, goodness, faithfulness, gentleness, <u>self-control</u>; against such things there is no law."

D. THE FOURTH REASON GOD GIVES US HIS LOVING COMMANDS IS SO THAT OUR DIGNITY WILL BE PRESERVED.

1. *What is dignity?*

DIGNITY *is the sense of nobility, worthiness, and honor that God puts in every man. It is an understanding that man has, that for some reason man is more than just an animal. God, within His nature, has nobility and dignity--He has created man in His own image. Man's awareness of dignity results from his being created in the image of God.*

2. *Satan's goal for man.*

    a. Satan enjoys manipulating people into the belief that they are basically run by passion and by glandular secretion, rather than by the power of God. Satan's desire is to make a mockery of man's honor.

    b. Look at the way Satan tried to convince Jesus to live by his own bodily needs alone:

Matthew 4:1-4 (Living Bible)
"Then Jesus was led out into the wilderness by the Holy Spirit, to be tempted there by Satan. For forty days and forty nights he ate nothing and became very hungry. Then Satan tempted him to get food by changing stones into loaves of bread. "It will prove you are the Son of God," he said. But Jesus told him, "No! for the Scriptures tell us that bread won't feed men's souls: obedience to every word of God is what we need."

PERSONAL APPLICATION:

Satan will come to you saying, "Hey, your passions are the most important thing there is. You had better get all the kicks you can to satisfy these desires while you still have them." You are more than that which your glands dictate. You are a person with honor, self-worth and the ability to love. God wants you to live in honor.

3. _Sex and dignity go hand-in-hand._

    a. Because they involve the most personal parts of both our bodies and our inner persons, sex and dignity are linked. Each of us places a heavy value on our physical bodies and our sexual needs. When we misuse our bodies by submitting to raw sexual desires, we degrade them and actually tear at our personal worth. _The Bible speaks of this:_

I Corinthians 6:18-20 (Living Bible)
"That is why I say to run from sex sin. No other sin affects the body as this one does. When you sin this sin it is against your own body. Haven't you yet learned that your body is the home of the Holy Spirit God gave you, and that He lives within you? Your own body does not belong to you. For God has bought you with a great price. So use every part of your body to give glory back to God because He owns it."

✳ From verses 19 & 20, why do you think God puts such high value on our bodies? _____

(Our bodies are the home of the Holy Spirit. God paid dearly to obtain them and to redeem them from death.)

    b. Sexual activity has a great effect upon us personally--deeply. We strive to maintain proper dignity and self-worth. When we share intimately with another, we give part of that dignity away, expecting something in return--something lasting, rewarding, meaningful, and of value. When in return we do not receive a relationship of meaning, we sense that our dignity has been ripped up and that something is desperately messed up and wrong.

GOD SAYS:

Proverbs 4:23
"Watch over your heart with all diligence For from it flow the springs of life."

WE NEED TO SEE THAT GOD HOLDS US ACCOUNTABLE FOR THE DIGNITY OF THE PERSON WE DATE. REALIZE THAT YOU CAN EITHER CONTRIBUTE POSITIVELY OR NEGATIVELY TO THAT PERSON. THERE NEEDS TO BE A BALANCE BETWEEN OUR PHYSICAL INVOLVEMENT AND THE COMMITMENT TO THAT PERSON.

> ## GOD IS NOT CRUEL
>
> God is neither stupid nor cruel. His commands are both wise and loving. He loves you and I so much that He wishes for each of us to be true lovers, and have a stable marriage as we live our lives in dignity and honor.

V. Three basic questions concerning sex.

Q. "I see a lot of beautiful, sexy women every day; is simply looking at them lusting?"

A. "Jesus Christ spoke very clearly concerning lust in Matt 5:27-28; 'The law of Moses says you shall not commit adultery. But I say: "anyone who even looks at a woman with lust in his eye, has already committed adultery with her in his heart."'" (Living Bible)

Jesus did not take lusting lightly. Yet, it is important to understand that a look is not lust. You do not have complete control over the people who pass your way each day. Here is a three-part test that will help you determine whether your look is a look of lust:

1. Did you welcome the temptation? If you are out looking for women, with the purpose of staring her down and letting your imagination run wild, then you are asking for trouble.

2. Did you set your whole mind to thinking about the temptation? Lust is able to get a grip on you when you visualize erotic relationships that have nothing to do with commitment at all.

3. If you knew you would not get caught, would you actively seek to fulfill your thoughts with that person? If so, you are deep in lust because you are about to turn your thoughts into action. If you have answered "yes" to any of these tests, there is a good possibility that you have flunked and are in the grips of lust. A method of escape is found in Job 31:1 - "I made a covenant with my eyes, how then shall I gaze upon a virgin?"

Q. *"We didn't plan to, but my boyfriend and I have gone too far. How did we get into this situation?"*

A. *"You probably were not aware of the steps to sexual arousal. God has designed us so that one sexual activity will lead to another, climaxing in intercourse. This chart shows the progression:"*

- *holding hands*
  - *kissing*
    - *super-kissing*
    - *caressing*
      - *super-caressing*
      - *so on...*
        - *more intense so on...*
        - *sexual intercourse*

You probably progressed down the ladder one step at a time until you found yourself at the level where you are now. You and your boyfriend need to decide where you are going to stop. Maybe then you won't even want to start!

Q. *"If my girlfriend and I have gone too far, what are some positive steps we can take to solve this situation?'*

A. *"Some possible solutions are:"*

1. Start talking about the problem with your girlfriend. It is easy to suppress guilt feelings for awhile for fear that the relationship will fall apart. If the sex problem is not dealt with, your relationship will fall apart.

2. Both people must agree that what they have done is wrong and against their moral standards. If one or the other does not feel there has been a violation when there actually has been, there is not yet hope for a cure. If you value God's thoughts you will get out of the relationship.

3. Ask yourself the sobering question, "What else do we do on a date besides making-out?" You need to establish common interests and reasons for dating apart from your sexual "turn-on." Sex is not a sufficient catalyst to hold a relationship together.

4. Plan your dates together before they happen. Poor planning of a date can easily lead to sexual activity, sometimes because of boredom. You may want to plan some double dates, day time dates, dates that will allow you to do more than look into each other's eyes--spiritually encouraging dates. If you have done all that you had planned to do by 11:00 p.m., say goodnight.

5. Pray together. Pray so that God and your partner know that there is a struggle in this area. Try praying before the date for guidance, rather than asking a prayer of forgiveness at the end of the date.

6. Decide together that if you cannot stop what you are doing, you will break off the relationship. It is better to have tears now, than deep scars in the years to come.

NOTES

The importance of understanding
DATING
Discussion 7

THRILLS AND CHILLS.

Each of us, at one time or another, has thought about the possibility of becoming involved in dating. The activity of dating thrills some, terrifies others, makes some laugh or even cry. Our present date life can greatly effect our future. It has the potential for controlling a large part of our thoughts and actions. God has a design for dating which will make us truly happy. Although the Bible does not have specific information about dating as such, it does give us standards and crucial guidelines for having successful relationships with those of the opposite sex. From these standards we are able to draw His goals for dating.

LET'S CONSIDER GOD'S GOALS FOR DATING...

...and some of the qualities you will want to look for in a dating partner.

I. *GOD'S #1 GOAL FOR US IS THAT WE ALLOW HIM THE FREEDOM TO CONTROL THIS AREA OF OUR LIVES. HIS DESIRE IS THAT WE TURN OUR ENTIRE DATE-LIFE AND FUTURE MARRIAGE PLANS OVER TO HIM.*

✳ *Is God in control of your relationship in dating?*

✳ *If He is, how do you know that He is in charge of your relationship?*

✳ *If God is not in control of your dating, how would it change things if He was?*

IT IS EASY...

...for us to allow our dating experience and dreams of marriage to have total freedom for dominating our lives. When this thinking controls most of our thoughts and actions, there is often little or no room for God and His guidance in our lives.

A. _It is absolutely impossible to have a truly successful dating relationship without Jesus Christ in complete control._

1. Conflict will result when a person pursues a relationship with a guy or girl _more_ than he/she pursues a relationship with Jesus Christ. It is important that you do not allow yourself to be misled in this area. Your first goal in life is not to have a good date life or even get married, but rather it must be to love God with all your heart. It is only when we pursue Christ and His ways that all of our endeavors in life will take on proper perspective.

Matthew 6:33
"But seek first His kingdom, and His righteousness; and all these things shall be added to you."

✳ As you think about dating, how does the phrase, "all these things shall be added to you" apply? _____

_____

✳ Is Jesus Christ your Lord, Saviour and best friend? _____ YES

YOUR DATE CAN'T MEET YOUR NEEDS.

We cannot expect the people we date to fulfill those needs in our lives that only Jesus Christ can meet. Don't depend on your boyfriend or girlfriend to do for you what only Jesus Christ can do. We can never expect our friends to give us spiritual power. Spiritual power can only come as the result of a direct relationship with Jesus Christ.

✳ Can you honestly say to God...

Psalm 73:25-26
"Whom have I in heaven but thee? And besides thee I desire nothing on earth. My flesh and my heart may fail, but God is the strength of my heart, and my portion forever!"

2. It is easy for us to slip into panic, feeling that God is not going to give us the right date or marriage partner. We often feel that God has somehow forgotten us.

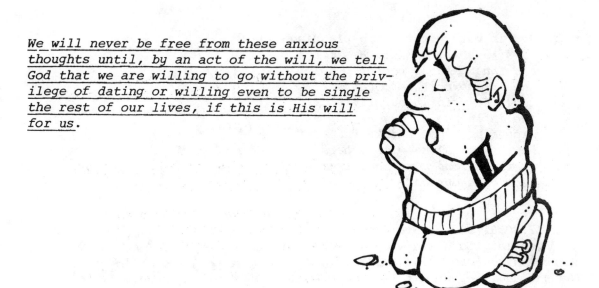

We will never be free from these anxious thoughts until, by an act of the will, we tell God that we are willing to go without the privilege of dating or willing even to be single the rest of our lives, if this is His will for us.

We must have the same attitude concerning our dates and future marriage that Job had as he faced his life's decisions:

Job 23:14
"For He performs what is appointed for me, And many such decrees are with Him."

STOP!

Before moving on through this discussion, consider the following question: "Would you be willing to allow Christ to take control of your entire 'love life?'" Christ promises that He will control this area of your life if you will allow Him. If He is in command of this area, then His promise to you is seen in the following verse:

Psalm 84:11 (Living Bible)
"For Jehovah God is our Light and our Protector. He gives us grace and glory. No good thing will He withhold from those who walk along His paths."

II. *GOD'S PLAN IS THAT WE HAVE THE PROPER REASONS AND MOTIVES IN DATING.*

✳ *What do you think your reasons for dating are?* _____

_____

✳ *Do you think God has a reason for you to date?* _____

A. *Reasons for dating:*

1. We should desire to date so that we as individuals may grow.

a. God is very creative in planning
ways to shape us into His image
and thus make us better people.
One of the most important
tools He uses in our lives is
the influence of other people
around us. God thinks that
how we get along with others
is the second-most important
factor in our lives.

Mark 12:30,31 (Living Bible)
"And you must love Him with all your
heart and soul and mind and strength.
The second is: You must love others as
much as yourself. No other commandments
are greater than these."

* What is the second-most important commandment?

<u>you must love others
as you do yourself.</u>

b. Being around other people can benefit you in these ways:
- learning more about who you are
- discovering your strengths
- finding out your weaknesses
- learning the areas of your life that need to become more
  Christ-like
- understanding the concept of giving

c. Having friends sharpens us to become the kind of people God
wants for His kingdom.

Proverbs 27:17 (Living Bible)
"A friendly discussion is as stimulating as the sparks that fly when
iron strikes iron."

IN DATING, TWO PEOPLE COME TOGETHER TO SHARE...

...with one another from their individual viewpoints. Since God has
created male and female with a masculine and feminine point of view,
each is a benefit to the other. A guy needs the feminine point of
view in his ear to help him more effectively relate to life, and a woman
needs to hear a more masculine point of view in order to relate to
life from a broader perspective. Therefore, a guy will grow emotionally, socially and spiritually from spending time with the right kind
of girls. A girl will grow emotionally, socially and spiritually if
she also stays around the right type of guys. Dating gives us this
opportunity for growth.

2. The second reason for dating is so that we may contribute to
the growth of another person.

2. Each person we date has special needs that God desires to meet. Dating offers us an opportunity to work with God, letting God work through us, in fulfilling some of these needs.

Romans 14:19
"So then let us pursue the things which make for peace and the building up of one another."

✳ What are some ways that you can build up the person you date?

_____

3. Dating also enables one to get ready for the right marriage partner.

2. Marriage is a great responsibility with a lifelong commitment. A successful marriage takes hard work and much compromise. Dating gives an opportunity to learn how to develop patterns of living that will help us in our future marriage. We also learn which dating characteristics in others are compatible to us. God will allow tests in dating which will prepare us for the much larger tests of life(marriage). It is important to realize that our date-life can deeply affect our marriage.

GOD TAUGHT THIS PRINCIPLE TO JEREMIAH:
Jeremiah 12:5
"If you have run with footmen and they have tired you out, Then how can you compete with horses? If you fall down in a land of peace, How will you do in the thicket of Jordan?

IF YOU are EXPERIENCING BaD attITUDES...
...that have a negative effect on your dating relationship, you better realize that there is a chance they might affect your marriage. If it is hard for you to get along with people while you date, do you think it will be easier when you marry?
As we date, God will reveal weaknesses that need to be surrendered to Him. He will also broaden our perspective as to the type of person we might like to live with the rest of our lives.

It is God's desire that our dating will result in positive learning experiences for everyone we involve--and for we ourselves.

III. *BECAUSE OF HIS LOVE TOWARD US, GOD INSTRUCTS TRUE CHRISTIANS NOT TO DATE UNBELIEVERS (PEOPLE WHO DO NOT HAVE A PERSONAL RELATIONSHIP WITH JESUS CHRIST).*

A. *God's Word is clear when it speaks of what our motives should be as we date, and the type of individual with whom we should build such relationships. We may have previously formed opinions about dating non-Christians, but God's Word supercedes our feelings and gives us solid instruction that stands the tests of time and of circumstance.*

GOD CLEARLY STATES:

II Corinthians 6:14,15 (Living Bible)
"Don't be teamed with those who do not love the Lord, for what do the people of God have in common with the people of sin? How can light live with darkness? And what harmony can there be between Christ and the Devil? How can a Christian be a partner with one who doesn't believe?"

✳ *Do you think that when you spend time dating someone, you become somewhat of a team with that person?* _____

_____

✳ *If you are dating a person who's a non-Christian, what things do you have in common?*

✳ *Name some things you don't have in common.* _____

_____

BECAUSE GOD LOVES US...

Because of His love for us, God desires to have us focus our attention and energy on loving Him. Therefore, He wants our date life to help us focus on Him rather than turn our attention to something else.

GOD KNOWS THAT AN UNBELIEVER WILL NOT HELP FOCUS OUR ATTENTION ON HIM AND HIS WAYS.

The Bible clearly states what the unbeliever focuses upon for his
lifestyle:

Titus 3:3(Living Bible)
"Once we, too, were foolish and disobedient; we were misled by others
and became slaves to many evil pleasures and wicked desires. Our lives
were full of resentment and envy. We hated others and they hated us."

HERE IS JUST a TOKEN LIST OF WHERE a NON-CHRISTIAN'S HEAD REALLY IS :

* "foolish" - He/she is foolish because he does not find eternal
        values to be very important.

* "disobedient" - He/she is deeply rebellious toward God and has no
        power inside to really obey Him.

* "misled by others" - He/she usually hangs out with those who accept
        their rebellious ways, therefore reinforcing their foolishness.
        (This is why others may very easily get upset if you continue to
        speak of Christ, especially if their friends are nearby.)

* "slaves to many evil pleasures and wicked desire"--Evil pleasure
        and wicked desire is more than just sexual kicks; it includes
        any desire that blocks God out or goes against His ways. These
        may include:
        ● over-concern with popularily
          ● over-concern with money
            ● status
            ● cars
            ● selfcenteredness nope
            ● wasting hours on temporal things nope
            ● sex Bad nope
            ● drugs Bad nope
            ● alcohol nope
                    Bad

* "full of resentment and envy" - The unbeliever is open to all kinds
        of resentment and envy when somebody challenges his popularity,
        status, etc. This is because he doesn't have the Person of
        Christ in him to help him really love.

Ephesians 4:17-18
"This I say therefore, and affirm together with the Lord, that
you walk no longer just as the Gentiles also walk, in the
futility of their mind, being darkened in their understanding,
excluded from the life of God, because of the ignorance that
is in them, because of the hardness of their heart;"

The Bible clearly states what a true Christian should be focusing upon
for his lifestyle:

Philippians 4:8(Living Bible)
"Fix your thoughts on what is true and good and right. Think about
things that are pure and lovely, and dwell on the fine good things
in others. Think about all you can praise God for and be glad about."

* "true" - A Christian does not live in an illusory world. He sees
        things God's way, which is the way things really are.

✳ "good"--A Christian focuses his attention on what is constructive and healthy, so that life and eternity reflect lasting joy.

✳ "right"--A Christian knows that the wrong way of doing things may work for awhile, but always ends in pain. He knows of God's righteousness and wishes to follow it.

✳ "pure"--The Christ controlled Christian cares about the other person's dignity. Thus, he or she is constantly seeking to focus on others in a nondegrading and clean way.

✳ "dwell on the fine and good things in others" -- The Christian who is Christ-controlled could hate others, but he is learning to see people as lost, without God and in great need. Consequently, he/she is becoming more compassionate all the time.

THE CHRIST-CONTROLLED CHRISTIAN...

...has learned how to give God praise for everything. His trusting, positive attitude affects those around him, so that they can see Christ's control at the root of his attitude.

✳ After checking the focus of lifestyle of both the believer and the unbeliever, by which way of living would you rather be influenced?

ARE YOU RESPONDING TO THE RIGHT PERSON?

Realize that you soon begin to respond to the actions and thoughts of the one you are dating. God does not want us responding or copying worldliness and sin. He wants us to turn from sin and walk with those who are seeking Him and who will encourage us to do the same.

II Timothy 2:22
"Now flee from youthful lusts, and pursue righteousness, faith, love and peace, with those who call on the Lord from a pure heart."

ONCE WE HAVE MADE SURE...

...that God is controlling our date life and that we have the proper motives for dating, then we may begin to seek the type of person we feel would be right to date.

IV. GOD SHARES HIS COUNSEL WITH US RELATING TO THE QUALITIES THAT OUR DATING PARTNER SHOULD POSSESS.

HERE IS A LIST OF QUALITIES...

...that a woman should look for as she considers the man she desires to date:

✳ *He should be a man who seeks after God.*

- *If the guy you are dating is not actively seeking the will of Jesus Christ in every area of his life, it is impossible for you to have the joyful relationship God intends for you.*

- *No guy is perfect, but God is concerned that the primary thrust of a man's life is to know God in a deeper way.*

- *If your boyfriend can talk about everything under the sun except spiritual things--BE CAREFUL! A person will soon verbalize that which he feels inside.*

  1. If he tells you that in the future he will discuss spiritual things, when he knows you better--BEWARE!

  2. If he doesn't lead you in spiritual things now, while he's trying to win your heart, he certainly will not do it once he has won your heart.

- *If he continually badmouths other Christians because they're too strict, there is a possibility that he might have a rebellious spirit.*

KiNG DaviD WaS a MAN WHO SOUGHT AFTER GOD.

King David had some weaknesses, but he also had many qualities that a woman would want in a man. As David thought about the qualities that would build his character as a man, he came to the conclusion that to seek God was his highest priority.

Psalm 27:4(Living Bible)
"The one thing I want from God, the thing I seek most of all, is the privilege of meditating in His temple, living in His presence every day of my life, delighting in his incomparable perfections and glory."

✳ How much time does your boyfriend spend speaking of spiritual issues?

✳ In what ways does your boyfriend influence you to live for Christ?

✳ In what ways does your boyfriend express how God will fit into your future plans?

IT'S TOO EASY.

It is easy to be dating a man who knows Christ, but isn't developing the quality of seeking God. If you settle for this type of man, you will soon become frustrated and your deepest needs will not be met. Your deepest need is to seek God with all your heart. Whatever you do, make sure that your man is a true seeker of God.

✳ Is he a leader?

●God clearly says in His Word that men are to be the leaders in the male-female relationship. God has not made men superior to women, but has specifically assigned then this function in relationships as a part of His design.

Ephesians 5:22,23(Living Bible)
"You wives must submit to your husband's leadership in the same way you submit to the Lord. For a husband is in charge of his wife in the same way Christ is in charge of His body the church."

Obviously, the dating relationship is not marriage. One must realize, however, that personal qualities which will contribute to marriage must be developed long before the marriage ceremony. Therefore, a man should begin to lead in a dating situation so that he'll be preparing.

●What is a leader?

Luke 22:25-27(Living Bible)
"Jesus told them, 'In this world the kings and great men order their slaves around, and the slaves have no choice but to like it! But among you, the one who serves you best will be your leader. Out in the world the master sits at the table and is served by his servants. But not here! I am your servant.'"

THE TRUE LEADER...

...is a servant to the one he dates. He is the one who initiates and accepts primary responsibility for the dating relationship.

HERE ARE A FEW QUESTIONS...

...which might help you to discover whether or not your boyfriend is developing true leadership qualities:

- *Does your boyfriend order you to do things without first asking meaningful questions?*
- *Does your boyfriend truely listen to you on a date after asking meaningful questions?*
- *Does he make demands on you and then insinuate that you are dumb and without worth when you don't agree with him?*
- *Does your boyfriend respect your point of view?*
- *Is he pushy and defensive about his beliefs and opinions?*
- *Does he let you know how he feels about things in a kind way?*
- *When it comes to making a decision which concerns your relationship, does he ask your opinion and sometimes follow it?*

A leader takes responsibility for all areas of the dating relationship --including and especially the moral aspects.

- *What moral standards does your boyfriend have?*
- *Have you ever discussed these standards?*
- *Who initiates the moral standards in your relationship?*
- *Who protects the moral standards in your relationship?*

SOME GUYS LIKE TO...

...remove the responsibility for the sexual area of dating from themselves. They simply state that since they have little self-control, the girl should keep the date under control because, "I can't always hold myself back--you turn me on so much." But most guys have more self-control than they realize or are willing to admit. To give the girl the responsibility for sexual control in dating is a "leadership cop-out." It is a feeble attempt on the part of a guy to create a "gray area" over which he isn't responsible but she is, so that if they begin to go too far, it quickly becomes, "I'm really sorry but that's just an example of the kind of area I'm weak in." The real weakness of a guy who creates this situation successfully with his date is genuine moral weakness that is wrong!

God clearly gives guys his instructions concerning how they are to act toward the person they date.

I Timothy 5:2
"(Treat) the older women as mothers, and the younger women as sisters, in all purity."

✳ *Does he have the quality of thoughtfulness?*

●*Women have a need for attention. It is important that this need is met for them to be truly fulfilled. It is God's intention that men be thoughtful in their dealings with those of the opposite sex.*

I Peter 3:7 (Living Bible)
"You husbands must be careful of your wives, being thoughtful of their needs and honoring them as the weaker sex. Remember that you and your wife are partners in receiving God's blessings, and if you don't treat her as you should, your prayers will not get ready answers."

✳ *What should the man of God be thoughtful of in dealing with the weaker sex?* _____

MANY MEN FEEL...

...that it is not masculine to be sensitive to the needs of a woman. Jesus Christ was the most sensitive person who ever existed; He never emotionally trampled over anyone, yet He was a true, masculine man.

A THOUGHTFUL MAN:

●*Is sensitive to the feelings of the girl he is dating. He is aware that a woman may respond emotionally to what is said and therefore misinterpret his communication. The thoughtful man strives to make his actions true and clear. He will also take the time to clear up any misconceptions.*

●*He has the courage to admit his own weaknesses. He has learned well the instruction of the Lord which says, "Before honor comes humility" (Proverbs 15:33). He is not afraid to admit his loneliness, fears, needs and emotional pains. He is not afraid to admit when he is wrong or to seek forgiveness from the woman he dates.*

●*He is sensitive to the many details that are important to a woman. He knows she needs much encouragement in her hobbies and activities.*

●*He is quick to praise the positive qualities in a girl's life. "Praise her for the many fine things she does" (Proverbs 31:31a -LB).*

●*He is not threatened by the success of those around him. He is quick to give honor to one who deserves to receive it.*

●*He is slow to lose his patience when wronged, and gently corrects those who oppose his knowledge --even when he knows he is absolutely right!*
"God's people must not be quarrelsome; they must be gentle, patient teachers of those who are wrong. Be humble when you are trying to teach those who are mixed up concerning the truth. For if you talk meekly and courteously to them they are more likely, with God's help, to turn away from their wrong ideas and believe what is true" (II Timothy 2:24,25 -LB).

●*I Timothy 5:8*
"But if anyone does not provide for his own, and especially for those of his household, he has denied the faith, and is worse than an unbeliever."

Can you think of ways that your boyfriend has shown you real thoughtfulness? _____

_____

HERE iS a LIST OF QUALiTiES...

...that God wants a man to desire in the woman he would date:

✳ *Is she a woman who seeks after God?*

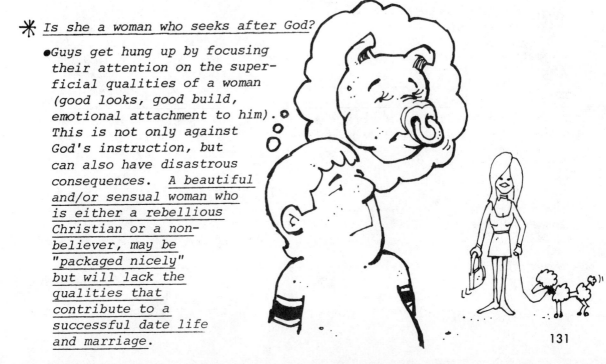

●*Guys get hung up by focusing their attention on the superficial qualities of a woman (good looks, good build, emotional attachment to him). This is not only against God's instruction, but can also have disastrous consequences. A beautiful and/or sensual woman who is either a rebellious Christian or a nonbeliever, may be "packaged nicely" but will lack the qualities that contribute to a successful date life and marriage.*

131

Proverbs 11:22 (Living Bible)
"A beautiful woman lacking
discretion and modesty is like
a fine gold ring in a pig's snout."

✳ What does it mean to lack discretion and modesty? _____

_____

● A guy should not feel guilty for being physically attracted to
his date. Yet, he better understand that a good figure or pretty
face is not to be the basis for dating a girl. God tells us the
qualities which contribute to a successful date life and future
marriage. He tells us the most important quality in a woman is
that of being a seeker after God.

Proverbs 31:30
*"Charm is deceitful and beauty is vain, But a woman who fears the
Lord, she shall be praised."*

```
┌──────────────────────────────────────────────────┐
│           SOME MEN THINK...                        │
│  ...that fine, womanly qualities such as being a   │
│  good cook, neat, able to sew, clean and tidy,     │
│  well dressed, supportive of him, etc., are the    │
│  most important qualities that he could find in    │
│  a woman.  While these are good and commendable    │
│  qualities, they are not the most important        │
│  qualities.                                        │
└──────────────────────────────────────────────────┘
```

Jesus taught us what the most important quality is--in a real life?
situation:

Luke 10:38-42
*"As Jesus and the disciples continued on their way to Jerusalem they
came to a village where a woman named Martha welcomed them in to her
home. Her sister Mary sat on the floor, listening to Jesus as He
talked. But Martha was the jittery type, and was worrying over the
big dinner she was preparing. She came to Jesus and said, 'Sir,
doesn't it seem unfair to you that my sister just sits here while
I do all the work? Tell her to come and help me!' But the Lord
said to her, 'Martha, dear friend, you are so upset over all these
details!'"*

✳ Was Martha doing something wrong when she desired to get her chores
done? _____

_____

THE IMPORTANCE OF A GOD-SEEKING WOMAN IN A MAN'S LIFE...

Most men have the inner desire to lead. They want to know that they are able to lead their relationship with a girl. When a man sees that a girl he is dating wants to seek God above everything else, he will feel compelled(if the relationship really matters to him) to lead in the direction she desires that it go. In this way, a woman can challenge a man to do exactly what God desires him to do. A godly woman with the right attitude can greatly affect a man who already knows Christ, by motivating him into a deeper walk with God.

Many women are eligible to date, but the man of God will follow His instruction as he decides which ones he's going to call.

Proverbs 31:10
"An excellent wife, who can find her? For her worth
is far above jewels."

✳ *Is she a woman with a gentle and quiet spirit?*

I Peter 3:3,4(Living Bible)
"Don't be concerned about the outward beauty that depends on jewelry, or beautiful clothes, or hair arrangement. Be beautiful inside, in your hearts, with the lasting charm of a gentle and quiet spirit which is so precious to God."

✳ *What is a quiet and gentle spirit?* _____

_____

HERE are SOME QUESTIONS...

...to help you discern whether your girlfriend is developing a quiet and gentle spirit:

- *Does your girlfriend complain a lot when she's around you?*
- *Does she argue a lot at home?*
- *Is she easily upset when circumstances don't go her way?*
- *Does she belittle you in front of others?*

BE VERY CAREFUL!

Be careful as you are dating a girl who complains alot and demands her own way. While God calls us to love all people, he wants us to be very careful about who we date seriously. You may be dating a contentious woman and that could be disaster for you.

Proverbs 21:19(Living Bible)
"Better to live in the desert than with a quarrelsome, complaining woman."

RACE OF LIFE

WHY IS IT IMPORTANT?

* Why is it important for a man to seek a woman who possesses a gentle and quiet spirit? The leading of a relationship is an awesome, difficult task. Any man who leads a relationship needs all the encouragement he can get. A man must continually look to God for the strength which will take him through the trials he faces as a leader. A wife is to help her husband be the type of leader God desires him to be. She is designed not only to help her husband, but also to encourage and respect him as God works through his life. When a woman becomes critical, quarrelsome and complaining, she becomes a distraction and an emotional drain on her husband. Instead of helping and encouraging him, she tears him down and discourages his will to lead. Therefore, it is of extreme importance that a man find a woman who has a gentle, understanding disposition.

REMEMBER:

Proverbs 12:4(Living Bible)
"A worthy wife is her husband's joy and crown; the other kind corrodes his strength and tears down everything he does."

You can be proud of a girlfriend or wife who is gracious and kind.

Proverbs 11:16a(Living Bible)
"...honor goes to kind and gracious women."

LeT's ViEW a FeW CHaRaCTeRiSTiCS...

...of the girl who possesses a quiet and gentle spirit:

✳ <u>*Her words are filled with kindness.*</u>

> *Proverbs 31:26 (Living Bible)*
> *"When she speaks, her words are wise, and kindness is*
> *the rule for everything she says."*

✳ <u>*She is an encourager.*</u>

> *Hebrews 10:24*
> *"Let us consider how to stimulate one another to love*
> *and good deeds."*

✳ <u>*She is modest.*</u>

> *Proverbs 11:22 (Living Bible)*
> *"A beautiful woman lacking discretion and modesty*
> *is like a fine gold ring in a pig's snout."*

●*What is modesty?*_____

✳ <u>*Is she one who is industrious?*</u>

Life is full of challenges and situations which call
for both creativity and hard work. There are qualities
that a girl can develop that will contribute to the
success of a dating relationship and marriage. It is
easy to go to extremes by either ignoring or over-
emphasizing such characteristics. God is concerned
that girls have the proper perspective toward these
attributes. He is not nearly as concerned that she
be able to perform in these areas of everyday life as
he is about her inner yieldedness to His work, as
shown in a willingness to: ●*seek Him*
                               ●*encourage others*
                               ●*show kindness*
                               ●*promote purity*
                               ●*respond in a gentle way*
                                 to situations of conflict

A FeW iNDuSTRiOuS QuaLiTYes...

Proverbs 31:13-16 (Living Bible)
"She finds wool and flax and busily spins it. She buys imported foods,
brought by ship from distant ports. She gets up before dawn to prepare break-
fast for her household, and plans the day's work for her servant girls.
She goes out to inspect a field, and buys it; with her own hands she
plants a vineyard."

✳ List some qualities that might be found in an industrious woman from the above verses. _____

_____

✳ Does your girlfriend see the importance of having some of these very qualities within her life? _____

Proverbs 14:1
"The wise woman builds her house, but the foolish tears it down with her own hands."

CAN YOU SAY OF YOUR GIRLFRIEND:

Proverbs 31:17a (Living Bible)
"...she is energetic, a hard worker"?

If not, she may be unwilling to work at acquiring those industrious qualities which will be absolutely necessary in her future.

REMEMBER, LOOK FOR THESE POSITIVE QUALITIES IN:

A GUY

●Does he love and seek God?
●Is he a leader?
●Is he thoughtful?

A GIRL

●Does she love and seek God?
●Does she have a gentle and quiet spirit?
●Is she industrious?

The importance of understanding
LOVE
Discussion 8

FEELINGS are WONDERFUL...

One of life's greatest influencing factors is human emotion. Our walk with God is often tested by many different strong emotions. God has interwoven feelings with our personalities for a reason, but at times our sin nature and lack of wisdom can cause feelings that are deceptive. The mature Christian is one who does not place his faith in his feelings, but rather ultimately says, "I choose to be led by God and His Word, no matter how I feel." Feelings are wonderful but, unless one is under the control of the Holy Spirit, they can be our worst enemy.

Proverbs 4:23
"Watch over your heart with all diligence, For from it flow the springs of life."

PERHAPS THE STRONGEST EMOTION...

...encountered is the one we sense when we think we are in love with someone of the opposite sex.

1. Have you ever dated someone who you felt was "the one for you?"

2. How did you feel when you thought you were in love?

3. Did you come to find out later that you were wrong?

4. Once you discovered that this one was not really "the one" for you, how did you feel?

LOVE AND MARRIAGE.

As we encounter a relationship with someone of the opposite sex and are overwhelmed with feelings of love toward that person, we need to watch for pitfalls. One important pitfall to avoid is the loss of objectivity. Objectivity is the ability to mentally evaluate things the way they really are, rather than being manipulated by the way we feel. Thousands of people have allowed their feelings to override their objectivity in making crucial decisions which can greatly affect their lives(sex before marriage, hasty engagements, premature marriage), only to find out later that they were not in love at all. Often this realization comes too late and leaves deep scars in the lives of those who have chosen to follow their emotions rather than their reasoning ability.

WHILE GOD HAS EMOTIONS...

...in a divine sense, His objectivity always determines the way He acts. He is the only Person Who makes decisions based upon a complete understanding of every situation. His love for us has caused Him to give, in His Word, clear guidelines which enable us to distinguish between genuine love and the emotional impulse of love (infatuation).

NOW LET'S GET INTO LOVE AND INFATUATION.

We'll communicate some tests which will enable us to be more objective as we desire God's leading in this crucial area of our lives.

INFATUATION

Infatuation is the emotional impulse of love. It is based on a superficial knowledge of the other person and has not faced the important tests of time and circumstances.

THE WORLD'S VIEW OF LOVE.

The world thinks of love as an intense, temporal feeling that comes upon two people who are "right for each other." These feelings become so strong that they conclude that they should get married. Since emotions have been the controlling factor in making their decisions, they become enslaved as a result of faulty reasoning. When these same feelings leave, they feel that love has fled them, leaving divorce as their only avenue of escape.

- Have you ever seen an advertisement that takes the infatuation view of love?
- Are there movies which contain attractive relationships based on the infatuation view of love?
- Are there any popular songs you've heard that communicate the infatuation viewpoint?

THIS ISN'T GOD'S VIEW.

It is not only possible, but probable, that those who do not know Jesus Christ are locked into the infatuation view of love. It is imperative that we understand that this view is not God's view.

LOVE is an emotional need and an act of the will in response to an intellectual evaluation of the other person's character.

Some people say "love is blind." The person who blindly denies the shortcomings of another person is clearly caught up in the infatuation viewpoint. Genuine love realistically looks at and deals with the weaknesses of another person in a non-judgmental, accepting way.

WHILE IT IS TRUE...

...that an infatuation view of love is only temporary and is not a sufficient foundation for a relationship, it is possible that a genuine love relationship could begin in the infatuation stage.

I. LET'S LOOK AT A FEW TESTS TAKEN FROM I CORINTHIANS 13, THE LOVE CHAPTER, WHICH IF VIEWED OBJECTIVELY WILL HELP US DETERMINE THE DIFFERENCE BETWEEN LOVE AND INFATUATION.

A. "LOVE IS PATIENT" --I Corinthians 13:4

Infatuation hurries to become more involved romantically, so that the intense feelings may be kept alive.

139

Infatuation is in a <u>super-big rush</u> for:

- *security(assurance that the other person will not leave you)*

- *acceptance(being accepted just as you are)*

- *affection(an aroused feeling of intimacy due to some form of sexual activity*

- *adventure(seeking and enjoying new experiences together)*

GETTING BURNT.

A problem that infatuation and "the big hurry" syndrome often cause is, a burnt-out relationship. Once these areas of emotional need are filled and the relationship becomes more predictable, boredom sets in. The dangers of the "infatuation rush" is that we will say and do things which keep the intense romantic feeling alive only for a short while. These things are based on very little true facts about the person. <u>God wants us to be very careful of what we might romantically say to another, until we have had more time to exchange information regarding each other, and regarding the relationship itself.</u>

Proverbs 18:13(Living Bible)
"What a shame --yes how stupid to decide before knowing the facts."

SINCERE LOVE IS PATIENT, *it will take time to know the other person and his true character. If you feel that you are in love, time is on your side --<u>time is your best friend.</u>*

✳ *You will need time to find out some things about your boyfriend or girlfriend.*

　✳ *Is he/she patient or does he/she lose his/her temper? (You probably won't find this out after just a few dates.*

　✳ *How does he/she react when you let him/her down?*

✳ *How does he/she react when he/she doesn't get her own way?*

AND SOME MORE QUESTIONS...

✳ *Does he/she know all of you, or only one side of your personality?*

✳ *How does he/she respond to his/her parents? (His/her basic attitudes toward his/her parents can greatly affect his/her attitudes toward you.)*

✳ *Is this person orderly or sloppy? (This will prove to be a more important question in marriage than you might think!)*

✳ *How does he/she respond to his/her parents? (Their basic attitudes toward their parents can greatly affect their attitudes toward you.)*

* Does he/she make good conversation, or do you trust the silence of the romance to sustain you? (You need to remember that one of the biggest problems facing modern marriage is _boredom_.)

* Is this person lazy or hardworking? (A warm feeling is fine, but it won't put bread on the table or clean clothes in the closet.)

* Can the relationship last without sexual activity? (Never trust sex to mean anything positive if you experiement with it premaritally, so far as your relationship is concerned; never trust sex to keep your relationship going.)

* What does this person think about God? (Good looks and personality are fine, but they won't help develop a deeper walk with God.)

IT Takes Time...

...to answer these questions. _One word of advice:_ While dating a person, engage yourself in a variety of different activities that will put you and your partner in many realistic, true-to-life situations. This will give you a chance to check both the actions and the reactions of the two of you amidst many pressures and circumstances. Here is a rule that we need to think on often: _Love is always a growing process, and growth always takes time_. Give yourself the time to grow; love demands it.

"I'M GOING To CHANGE THIS PERSON"

Infatuation often tries to change the basic personality and lifestyle of the partner in order to fit your own stereotype of what the person "ought to" be. Perhaps you have heard someone say, "I really like this person, but there is about 20% of him that rubs me the wrong way, and I'm going to change him."

HERE are SOME QUALiTIES YOU MiGHT THiNK YOU NEED TO CHANGE iN THE PERSON YOU are SERiOUS aBOUT:

- too talkative
- too quiet
- seldom punctual
- lazy

- dominant
- indecisive
- self-centered
- fickle

- jealous
- overly-sensitive
- impatient

IT iS iMPOSSiBLE...

...for you to change someone through your own efforts. Change in your partner's life comes through his submission to the work of the ¬ie Holy Spirit. Pressuring someone to change is a dangerous activity. This pressure is both damaging and immature, and is certainly not a characteristic of genuine love.

Aggressive, dominant behavior toward your partner and attempting to help them perform up to your expectations, will have the following negative results in their lives. They will:

- develop insecurity

- be easily threatened

- fear rejection

- begin to worry

- have a low self-image

- focus their attention on what they can do for themselves, rather than on what God can do through them

WHEN YOU START A NEW RELATIONSHIP...

...ask yourself the question, "Am I putting this person on a performance scale to see how they measure up to my own expectations?" Don't be guilty of trying to put someone into a new mold in your relationships.

TRUE LOVE

True love learns to accept the partner just as he is, along with all his weaknesses. God demonstrates His love for us by being slow to lose patience. Because of His love, He does not see us as objects to be manipulated, nor would He ever belittle us. God does not keep a list of our wrongs, using them against us. Therefore, we can be secure in God's love for us and its constancy.

I John 4:18-19 (Living Bible)
"We need to have no fear of someone who loves us perfectly; His perfect love for us eliminates all dread of what he might do to us. If we are afraid, it is for the fear of what He might do to us, and shows that we are not really convinced that He really loves us. So you see, our love for Him comes as a result of His loving us first."

GOD WANTS TO SHOW HIS LOVE, THROUGH US, TO THE PERSON WE ARE DATING!

Love says to your partner...

"...I accept you just the way you are--even when:

⁕ *you look good; when you look bad."*

⁕ *you move as quickly as I like; when you move too slowly."*

⁕ *you smell good; when you smell bad."*

⁕ *you are in a good mood; when you're irritated."*

⁕ *you are on time; when you are late."*

⁕ *you are self-motivated; when you are lazy."*

⁕ *you are sensitive; when you are insensitive."*

⁕ *you are giving; when you are selfish."*

⁕ *you are fun to be with; when you are a drag."*

ASK THIS QUESTION:

As you find yourselves becoming more serious about your dating relationship, ask this question; "Could I live with this person, just the way he is, for the rest of my life?"

B. "LOVE IS KIND" --I Corinthians 13:4

Infatuation tends to quickly forget the importance of doing
kind deeds for the partner. When you first date a person whom
you really like, it seems easy to do kind, creative deeds which
show your affection. Genuine love will prove itself through
continued, creative service to the partner.

Here's a LIST...

...of some things you might do to show your partner kindness:

- spend time with his/her parents

- call the person on the phone

- be a patient listener

- send letters and cards in the mail

- have a willingness to run errands

- send flowers to her

- make cookies for him

- be willing to spend time at places which, or with friends whom,
  you may not particularly enjoy, if that would please your
  partner

A problem with the relationship that is based on infatuation is the
inconsistency of unselfish giving. _This type of a relationship begins
to fizzle out and become boring as it becomes hard work, rather than a
pleasure to serve the other person._ While love is a wonderful thing,
it is silly to delude ourselves into thinking the relationship is real
love, unless we are willing to give, give, and give some more. If you
have become sporadic in your giving to your partner, it would be wise
to check your relationship for signs of infatuation.

Love is concerned...

...that the other person grows as an individual. It will strive to
deepen the life of the one being dated. Kindness seeks creative
avenues by which one can contribute to the other's life.

Check your creativity by answering these questions:

* What activities do you do together? (Tennis, bike riding, horseback
riding, studying, shopping, spending time with underprivileged kids,
washing the car.)

* What projects could you do together that would help the other person
grow? (Discussing and evaluating your friendships with others, studying
the Bible together, memorizing Scripture, praying together, sharing your
faith together, visiting old folks homes, leading Bible study together,
jogging, double dating in order to meet the other couples' needs,
reading a book together.)

LOVE TAKES WORK

To develop giving activities and projects for dating relationships takes much effort. When you do get married, realize that the work continues if your relationship is to have meaning.

C. "LOVE IS NOT JEALOUS" - *I Corinthians 13:4*

Infatuation is easily threatened and therefore is possessive and insecure. A new relationship founded on infatuation has not yet faced the test of time. This relationship is based on emotion. A person who is caught up in infatuation feels that his new-found relationship requires hours of time with constant attention in order to make the dating worthwhile. Because of this, if you are caught up in infatuation, you can become hostile and distressed over any person or activity which may deprive you of this precious time with your partner.

JEALOUSY IS A STRONG AND VICIOUS EMOTION...

...because it is a reaction to the potential violation of our dearest possessions! God is seriously against the harmful effects of this:

Proverbs 27:4 (Living Bible)
"Jealousy is more dangerous and cruel than anger."

✳ *Why do you think jealousy is more dangerous and cruel than anger?*

_____

✳ *Think of a time when you were extremely jealous.* _____

_____

✳ *What are some symptoms that would enable you to notice when you are jealous?* _____

_____

THE VERY MOMENT...

...that you detect jealousy within you, realize that you have been crippled by immature and self-centered emotions.

Mature love gives your partner the freedom to develop as a person apart from you.

✻ A dating relationship is made successful by two people with differing personalities, backgrounds, and insights, sharing with one another all about who they are, what they've done, and what they dream for the future. While two people should and do grow from time spent together, they must also have other relationships which will cause them to grow while they are apart from each other.

> ## POSSESSIVENESS AND JEALOUSY
> Possessiveness and jealousy over your dating partner will deprive him of activities and people who could contribute to his development as a person. _This is not love, but is; self-centeredness on your part._

✻ Real love asks the question, "How can I help my boyfriend or girlfriend grow into a better person apart from me?"

YOU SHOULD SAY...

"...I care about you, _but_:

--there are some hobbies and activities you need to be involved in without me;"
--there are some nights that you need to spend with your family;"
--there are times that you need to spend with other friends;"
--there are times you need to be alone--to think, read and write without me;"
--you need to build your relationship with God alone, apart from involvement from me all the time."

REMEMBER:

Your girlfriend or boyfriend is not your possession, but is a gift from God. God desires that you, by serving that person, encourage him to become the most dynamic, positive Christian possible. _Set your partner free to do this by not being possessive or jealous._

D. "LOVE IS NOT PROVOKED"

I Corinthians 13:5

Infatuation is based on emotion and is hard pressed to stand up under the scrutiny of tough analysis and disagreement. The infatuated person thinks it is very important to keep the intense feeling of love alive; consequently, the rough edges and weaknesses are often shunned or covered over. Honesty involves being realistic, facing the facts the way they are. It does not romanticize life's situations, but protrays them realistically.

TRUE HAPPINESS   is obtained more easily when life situations are faced and dealt with openly and honestly.

HERE ARE SOME QUESTIONS THAT WILL HELP YOU AND YOUR PARTNER DISCERN WHETHER OR NOT YOUR RELATIONSHIP IS REALISTIC AND HONEST:

✳ *Are there weaknesses in your life that you keep from your partner, fearing that if he or she found out it would end your relationship?*

✳ *Are there things that you would like to do(date others, join a club) but fear sharing them with your partner, lest your relationship end?*

✳ *Are there "controversial subjects" that you would like to share but avoid for fear an argument will result?*

✳ *Does your partner have weaknesses in the areas of attitude or behavior that you would like to talk about, but are afraid of a "blow-up" in your relationship?*

✳ *Are there certain weaknesses which permeate your entire relationship, things that really bother you, but that you are afraid to mention for fear of losing the relationship?*

If you answered "yes" to any of these questions, then your dating relationship is in need of more honesty and objectivity.

ANOTHER MEANS TO WEIGH THE QUALITY OF YOUR LOVE...

...is the "disagreement test."

HOW DO YOU HANDLE DISAGREEMENTS?
It is easy to get along when you agree, but the real test of your love is linked to how you react when you face disagreement with each other.

Some immature ways to handle disagreement...

- *responding with "I just don't want to talk about it"*
- *making a big joke out of it (laughing it off)*
- *pouting or sulking*
- *the old silent treatment*
- *feeling, "I'm going to remember this incident and use it on him/her later against him/her, to teach him/her a lesson."*

MATURE LOVE WILL USE DIFFICULT SITUATIONS TO BECOME STRONGER.

Real love is determined to succeed; it centers in an understanding of these concepts:

●_Every friendship will encounter shaky times. Love is based on the knowledge that running from these hard times only makes the situation worse, not better. Real love uses the rough times to get stronger._

●_Love knows that there is an art to dealing with disagreement. Failure to get along with others can be one of the most crippling weaknesses in life. Love practices being open and honest and will respect the view of another._

●_Love has a desire to truly know the other person. Its honesty also gives the other the freedom to discover and explore it's true self. Love says that the two of us can face our weaknesses together._

E. "LOVE DOES NOT SEEK IT'S OWN" --I Corinthians 13:5

Infatuation deceives one into thinking that he is meeting the needs of the dating partner, when actually his own needs are being selfishly met, and not the partner's at all--or only incidentally to his own.

Acts 20:35
"In everything I showed you that by working hard in this manner you must help the weak and remember the words of the Lord Jesus, that He himself said, 'It is more blessed to give than to receive.'"

To be emotionally stable and healthy, your emotional needs must be met. How are you accomplishing that goal in your partner? The Bible clearly teaches that we are to enter a relationship with a giving attitude, not concentrating on what we can get.

GIRLS WILL SEEK GUYS FOR MANY REASONS...

1. A girl might meet a guy and say, "I have met the right one; he meets all my needs, I am in love." This girl might be in love, but, then again, she might be "in love with security." (Security is a wonderful thing, but be sure you are in love with the <u>person</u>, not with something he can give.)

2. A girl may be in love with attention; while attention is important, it certainly is not the guy himself. You will not be marrying a concept (attention) and manner, but rather the person--with or without his manner.

3. A girl may be in love with the status that the dating partner brings. A sense of accomplishment comes when we know we are cared for by someone of the opposite sex, but be careful that it does not take the place of your genuine love for him as a person.

IF YOU ARE CONTEMPLATING MARRIAGE...

...believing that you are in love, answer these questions honestly:

✳ Regardless of the mood my marriage partner might be in, would I be willing to give up half my time, the rest of my life, to be with him/her?

✳ Would I be willing to give even more time if we were to have a child?

✳ Am I willing to give up the majority of my independence?

✳ Am I willing to give up the money I earn for the sake of my family?

✳ Am I willing to become vulnerable to heartbreak? (Here you must remember that love is rewarding but is also demanding.)

IMPORTANT!

<u>Realize that a large part of love is "giving up" yourself for others, rather than getting for oneself.</u> (Stop and think about this 1 minute.)

GUYS HAVE A TENDENCY TO FALL IN LOVE...

...with physical appearance, rather than the real inner person. Physical attraction to your date is important, but physical attraction is not love.

THESE QUESTIONS WILL HELP YOU...

...to discern your attitude towards the physical attraction of your partner, if you are a guy:

＊ Once married, do you think her good looks will hold the relationship together through trying times?

＊ If you become upset at her for something she has done to you, will her good looks help quiet your anger?

＊ Do you think your girlfriend appreciates a compliment more for her good looks, or for her personality?

＊ If your girlfriend encountered an accident which left her physically scarred, would you still be able to tell her that you love her?

＊ If you had to spend hours talking to her on the phone rather than seeing her physically, would you get bored?

REMEMBER:

Some decisions in life are of greater importance than others. The decision of whom you will love and marry is perhaps more influential to your life's happiness than any other single decision. We desperately need God's wisdom and guidance and direction as we meet people of the opposite sex--people with whom there will be great attraction going both ways! Ask Him to show you what role you are to play in the lives of these people. Trust that God will clearly indicate to you which one of these people will potentially be your life's partner.

Proverbs 3:5-6
"Trust in the Lord with all your heart, and do not learn on your own understanding. In all your ways acknowledge Him, and He will make your paths straight."

The importance of
CLEARING THE MIND
Discussion 9

IT ALL APDS UP.

Each one of the many thoughts which cross your mind in the course of an average day, no matter how trivial or mundane, detracts a particular amount of your attention from God--if it isn't a spiritually rooted thought. Furthermore, God provides us with a sizeable amount of information regarding His relationship to our thought life. A pass taken through the Bible in search of the words "mind," "think," and "thought" would reveal many occurrences of each.

Psalm 139:2 (Living Bible)
"You know when I sit or stand. When far away you know my every thought."

IDEAS CAN GRIP US.

God knows that thought is the root of action. The more we think on a subject, the tighter it grips us and determines what we become. We cannot avoid the projection of our thoughts into action. If a person's mind dwells long enough on any single idea, that idea will affect the person's behavior.

Proverbs 23:7
"For as he thinks within himself, so he is."

TAKE INVENTORY OF YOUR THOUGHT LIFE...

* What fraction of your thinking would fall into the category of worry?

* What thoughts occupy your mind as you go to sleep at night?

* What thoughts come to you first thing in the morning?

* What fraction of your thoughts are impure thoughts?

* How much time do you spend thinking about:

- your job
- your car
- your sister
- your brother
- your boyfriend
- your girlfriend
- the hot date Friday nite
- homework

- athletics
- club activities
- sex
- yourself
- your sin
- clothes
- grades
- parents
- God

JESUS SAID...

Mark 7:21-23 (Living Bible)
"For from within, out of men's hearts, come evil thoughts of lust,
theft, murder, adultery, wanting what belongs to others, wickedness,
deceit, lewdness, envy, slander, pride, and all other folly. All
these vile things come from within; they are what pollute you and
make you unfit for God."

THE MIND CAN DESTROY

Our minds, if not supervised by the Holy Spirit,
can and will destroy our lives as Christians.
God desires that our thoughts fall under His
protective supervision.

II Corinthians 10:5
"We are destroying speculations and every lofty thing raised up
against the knowledge of God, and we are taking every thought captive
to the obedience of Christ."

According to this verse, the total dominion of Jesus Christ over our
thought life is conceivable and even desirable.

King David knew the extent to which God desired control over his
thought life when he prayed:

Psalm 139:23-24
"Search me, O God, and know my heart; try me and know my anxious thoughts.
And see if there be any hurtful way in me, and lead me in the everlasting
way."

Because the mind bears such significance in the Christian life, Satan
does not hesitate to attack this area.

LET'S DISCUSS...

- how Satan wages war on the mind
- how we can achieve victory in our thought lives
- how to glorify God with our minds

I. THREE PRINCIPAL ANTAGONISTS CONSISTENTLY WAGE WAR ON THE MIND. THEY INCLUDE SATAN, THE WORLD, AND THE FLESH.

A. The attack by Satan may come in the form of continual discouragement, guilt, confusion, fear, self-pity, or any other frame of mind suited to distract us from a simple and pure devotion to Christ.

II Corinthians 11:3
"But I am afraid, lest as the serpent deceived Eve by his craftiness, your minds should be led astray from the simplicity and purity of devotion to Christ."

GOD DESIRES...

...that we set our minds on Jesus Christ. Satan desires that we set our minds on anything but Jesus Christ. Specifically cite potential distractions that Satan could use to cause you to deviate from God's desire for your thought life, i.e., intimate relationships with ungodly people, a job that keeps you from Christian fellowship, a ministry that keeps you so busy that time alone with God gets phased out.

...Intimate relationships, jobs and ministries--all are good and all are important. Yet, if these activities fill your mind to the extent that they squeeze out your devotion to Christ, you can bet that Satan is on the scene.

B. In addition to Satan himself, our thought lives are often influenced by sensory data gathered in the course of everyday life from the world, a world which is (in most cases) both ignorant of and hostile toward God.

Romans 12:2(Living Bible)
"Don't copy the behavior and customs of this world, but be a new and different person with a fresh newness in all you do and think. Then you will learn from your own experience how his ways will really satisfy you."

THE MASS MEDIA.

Particularly in America where the mass media pervades most every corner of our lives, our senses are constantly bombarded with various stimuli--all designed to fight their way into the forefront of our thought lives.

✳ *By what specific medium does the world have a particularly strong impact upon your thought life?*

_____

_____

_____

_____

A MIND NOT ALERT TO GOD...

...and full of His thoughts will fall subject to the manipulations of the world, resulting ultimately in a mind hostile to God's ways.

BUT GOD IS AWARE...

...of the daily influence over your minds by all kinds of thoughts and pictures over which you have no control. He knows these can lead you away from Him. <u>It is not God's intention for you to escape the world, fleeing to a less "mind-polluting" universe</u>. Jesus revealed this thought as He prayed to His father about His disciples:

John 17:15
"I do not ask thee to take them out of the world, but to keep them from the evil one."

IF GOD does not intend for us to escape the world and its mind polluting stimuli, it is only logical to conclude that He must have a method to combat these thoughts.

    C. *The attack by our own sin nature comes on, in addition to Satan and the world thought system. The old sin nature is that part of us which would heed sin rather than God. The Bible refers to it as the "flesh" or the "old man."*

Romans 8:6
"For the mind set on the flesh(our sin nature) is death - (wrong thinking, wrong existence), but the mind set on the Spirit(God at work in our lives) is life and peace."

OUR SIN NATURE WOULD HAVE OUR THOUGHTS BE OPPOSITE TO GOD'S THOUGHTS

GOD WOULD HAVE US DWELL ON:	OUR SIN NATURE WOULD HAVE US DWELL ON:
1. *"Whatever is true";He would have us consider thought systems that do not fail as time passes.*	1. *Whatever is a lie; our sin nature is deceitful and wants us to dwell on its lies about life and happiness.*
2. *"Whatever is honorable";God wants us to think on thoughts that bring dignity to ourselves and to others.*	2. *Whatever is dishonorable; our sin nature wants us to dwell on anything that degrades ourselves and others.*
3. *"Whatever is just";God wants us to think on anything that will help us to live right and help us to deal truthfully with others.*	3. *Whatever is unjust; our sin nature subtly wants us to dwell on anything that would cause us to deal wrongly with others.*
4. *"Whatever is lovely";God wants us to think on anything that causes acceptance of others (thoughts of understanding, kindness, love; think on the good in others).*	4. *Whatever is unlovely; our sin nature works on our minds to get us to think thoughts that do not show acceptance of others (envy, jealousy, bitterness, hate).*
5. *"Whatever is gracious";God wants us to think thoughts that he accepts. It is important for us to think thoughts that we would not be ashamed of if God heard (since He is aware of these thoughts anyway).*	5. *Whatever is ungracious; our sin nature wants us to think thoughts that would not be pleasing to God.*

Philippians 4:8
"Finally, brethren, whatever is true, whatever is honorable, whatever is right, whatever is pure, whatever is lovely, whatever is of good repute, if there is any excellence and if anything worthy of praise, let your mind dwell on these things."

II. *LET'S VIEW SOME POSITIVE STEPS THAT CAN HELP YOUR THOUGHT LIFE TO BE PRODUCTIVE FOR JESUS CHRIST.*

A. <u>Realize that your mind <u>can</u> be controlled by God.</u>

Your Sin Nature...

...which includes your thought life, has been crucified with Christ. Through Jesus' resurrection, we have received a new life which has the capacity to victoriously overcome the temptation to think impure thoughts.

I Corinthians 10:13 (Living Bible)
"But remember this--the wrong desires that come into your life aren't anything new and different. Many others have faced exactly the same problems before you. And no temptation is irresistable. You can trust God to keep the temptation from becoming so strong that you can't stand up against it, for He has promised this and will do what he says."

✳ *According to verse 13, is there any temptation(including the temptation to think impure thoughts) which is too strong for us to overcome?_____*

Because Christ Loves Us...

...so much, He promises us that He will guard our minds if we turn to Him.

Philippians 4:6,7
"Be anxious for nothing, but in
everything by prayer and supplication
with thanksgiving let your requests
be made known to God. And the
peace of God, which surpasses all
comprehension, shall guard your
hearts and minds in Christ Jesus."

✳ What is the result of the peace which Christ gives us? _____

_____

B. Part of the answer to a clean and powerful thought life is that
you have your mind renewed by God.

Romans 12:2
"And do not be conformed to this world, but be transformed by the
renewing of your mind, that you may prove what the will of God is,
that which is good and acceptable and perfect."

✳ According to verse 2, what is God's solution to the problem of our
unclean minds? _____

✳ What does "renewing the mind" mean? _____

_____

More and More of Him.

To have our minds renewed, we
need to deeply concentrate on
the life of Jesus Christ.

No greater life was ever lived
than Jesus Christ's. His example
and lifestyle were overwhelming.
To think deeply about Christ and
to imitate Him in our daily lives
is God's goal for us. The more we
think about Him, the greater effect
He'll have on us.

Philippians 2:5
"Have this attitude in yourselves which was also in Christ Jesus."

CHRIST'S WAY of thinking was unique. As we set our minds to think about Jesus Christ, we will be able to begin to think as He thought.

HERE'S A PROJECT...

...to help you think about Christ:

1. Take any passage in the gospels and examine the life of Christ.

2. Ask yourself such questions about this passage as"
   - How did Jesus respond to the people around Him?
   - In what ways was He sensitive to their individual needs?
   - How would you appraise Christ's conduct in this situation?
   - How were the words which He spoke appropriate to the need of the moment?
   - What was the result of Christ's work in that situation?

3. The outcome of answering these questions is that you will begin to think about the life qualities of Jesus Christ.

4. At this point, as you face situations around you, compare your conduct and attitudes to those of Christ. How could your attitudes become more like Christ's? What situation might you face this day that would allow you the opportunity to respond the way Christ did?

5. Take a 3 x 5 card and write down the outstanding attributes of Christ that could possibly apply to the situations you might face today. Let these thoughts of Christ and His actions continually dominate _your_ mind and actions.

6. Try this project with Mark 10:46-52

THEN AS YOU CONTINUE...

...to apply this project day by day, a change in your thoughts will result. A genuine desire to be like Jesus Christ will invade your mind. Remember the words in Hebrews 12:2,3 (Living Bible):

"Keep your eyes on Jesus, our leader and instructor. He was willing to die a shameful death on the cross because of the joy He knew would be His afterwards; and now He sits in the place of honor by the throne of God. If you want to keep from becoming fainthearted and weary, think about His patience as sinful men did such terrible things to Him."

C. Meditating on Scripture will bring our minds renewal. King David, a man after God's own heart, continually meditated on God's Word to strengthen his mind and deepen his walk with God.

Psalm 119:97
"Oh how I love Thy law. It is my meditation all the day."

WHEN TO MEDITATE

Verse	General Meaning	Application
"Sit in your home"	Anytime you're with your family or friends or alone at home	Doing dishes, getting ready for school, eating meals, cleaning house
"Walk by the way"	Anytime between destinations	Drive to school, walk to class, trip to store
"When you lie down"	At time of rest	Before falling asleep at a nap or at bedtime in the evening
"When you rise up"	After a time of rest	Start your day with studying His Word

GOD IS AWARE OF THE EXTREME DIFFICULTY...

...of our thinking on Him every second of every day. Yet, if we love Him, our minds will never be far from Him, and we will take times throughout the day and night to focus all our attention on Him. on Him.

III. *THE BENEFITS OF HAVING OUR MINDS RENEWED BY MEDITATION.*

A. <u>We will have victory over sin.</u>

THERE IS NO SHORT CUT

There isn't any short cut to developing pure thoughts. If you have developed unclean, negative thinking, then it will take time for God's Word to penetrate and clean your mind of the impurity that is already there. Only God's Word through the work of the Holy Spirit can do this.

Psalm 119:9-11 (Living Bible)
(9) "How can a young man stay pure? By reading Your Word and following its
(10) rules. I have tried my best to find You
*   --don't let me wander off from Your*
(11) instructions. I have thought much
*   about Your words, and stored them*
*   in my heart so that they could*
*   hold me back from sin."*

✳ *According to verse 11, can a superficial reading of God's Word be an effective deterrent to sin?*

WHAT IS MEDITATION?

It is a personal devotion which involves a deep, continual reflection on God and His Word. It involves the dwelling of one's thoughts upon how God's Word applies to our daily lives.

IT IS SILLY TO ASSUME...

...that we can quit thinking impure thoughts without exchanging them for God's thoughts. God offers an alternative to wrong thinking. He offers us truth which reveals His thoughts.

PREREQUISITE TO MEDITATION = MEMORIZATION

Before one can continually reflect on one of God's thoughts, he must first have that thought committed to memory.

Psalm 119:11(Living Bible)
"I have thought much about Your words, and stored them in my heart so that they would hold me back from sin."

KING DAVID WAS AN EXAMPLE FOR US

King David had a good reason for thinking bitter and anxious thoughts. People were slandering him with false accusations. It would have been easy for David to lie in bed and fret long into the night, allowing thoughts of revenge to captivate his mind. He did quite the opposite.

160

Psalm 119:78(Living Bible)
"Let the proud be disgraced, for they have cut me down with all their lies. But I will concentrate my thoughts upon Your laws."

✳ *What was David's response when people abused him?* _____

_____

WHEN TO MEDITATE.

The Bible tells us which are the best times to meditate:

Psalm 1:2
"But His delight is in the law of the Lord, And in His law he meditates day and night."

David felt that any time was a good time to meditate on God's Scripture. And the Bible gets even more specific as to when and where we can bring our minds under the control of Christ and concentrate deeply on God's ways:

Deuteronomy 6:6,7
"And these words, which I am commanding you today, shall be on your heart; and you shall teach them diligently to your sons and shall talk of them when you sit in your house and when you walk by the way and when you lie down and when you rise up."

✳ *What does it mean to diligently teach your sons those things which God has taught you?* _____

_____

WE WILL HAVE GREAT WISDOM.
Psalm 119:97-100(Living Bible)
"Oh how I love them, I think about them all day long. They make me wiser than my enemies, because they are my constant guide. Yes, wiser than my teachers, for I am ever thinking of your rules. They make me even wiser than the aged."

✳ *According to the above passage, if you seriously meditate on God's Word, it will:*

- *"make me wiser than my enemies"; God's Word will give you the ability to discern and judge soundly concerning that which is true or false, proper or improper. It will cause you to have much greater insights into situations than your enemies do.*

- *"wiser than my teachers"; Any teacher apart from God does not have true wisdom which leads to life and peace.*

- *"wiser than the aged"; Since God is eternal, He is therefore older than the aged. He knows more, is wiser and understands the past and future better than any living person.*

161

WE WILL HAVE PROSPERITY.

Psalm 1:1-3

(1) "How blessed is the man who does not walk in the counsel of the
    wicked, nor stand in the path of sinners, nor sit in the seat of
(2) scoffers! But his delight is in the law of the Lord, and in His
(3) law he meditates day and night. And he will be like a tree firmly
    planted by streams of water, which yield its fruit in its season,
    and its leaf does not wither; and in whatever he does, he prospers."

  According to verse 3, what happens to the work of those who meditate
on God's Word? _____

BEING STINGY AND CRUEL IS NOT GOD'S THING.

Help and prosperity go to those who love Him and meditate on His Word.

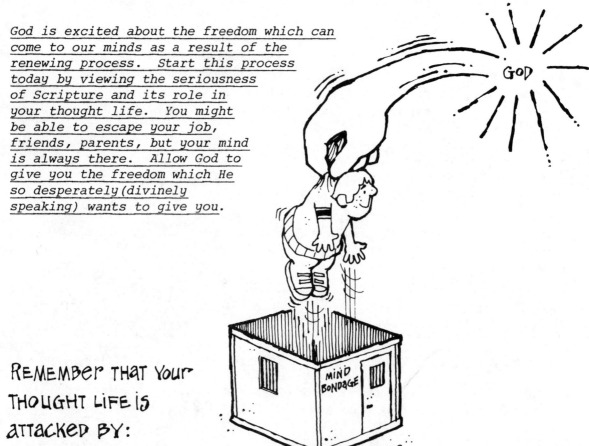

God is excited about the freedom which can
come to our minds as a result of the
renewing process. Start this process
today by viewing the seriousness
of Scripture and its role in
your thought life. You might
be able to escape your job,
friends, parents, but your mind
is always there. Allow God to
give you the freedom which He
so desperately (divinely
speaking) wants to give you.

REMEMBER THAT YOUR THOUGHT LIFE IS ATTACKED BY:

- Satan
- the world thought system
- your own sin nature

BECOME FAMILIAR WITH THE CONCEPTS...

...that will help you obtain a proper thought life:

- your thought life can be controlled by God's power
- it is important to have our minds renewed day to day by God
- one method of renewal is Scripture meditation and memorization

The importance of dealing with
TEMPTATION
DiSCUSSiON 10

Each Christian is involved in an intense spiritual warfare. As you strive to live for Christ, you will face great temptation to disobey God and to do things "your" way.

✻ Do you know why you are locked into a battle with Satan and your own rebellious sin nature?

_____

✻ Do you know why Satan is out to cause trouble in your life? *Yes*

✻ Are you aware that there is a world thought-system directly opposing God's ways, and therefore has directly challenged you?

_____

✻ Are you sensitive to the amount of rebelliousness within your own heart? _____

_____

✻ WHY IS THERE A WAR BETWEEN SATAN AND YOU?

It is because you have left his "team" and joined God's.

Colossians 1:13
"For He(God) delivered us from the domain of darkness, and transferred
us to the Kingdom of His beloved Son."

✴ What domain did we once belong to? __Darkness__

✴ Into what kingdom have we been transferred? __Of his beloved__
__Son. (Jesus)__

"THAT'S AN INSULT!"

You have insulted Satan
and his philosophy by
leaving his team. Satan
desires to deceive
each person by leading
him to think that he does
not need to be depen-
dent on God for genuine
happiness and fulfillment.
Satan is continually attempting to persuade man
that rebellion against God
leads to satisfaction in life.
When we accept Christ into our lives,
putting complete dependence upon Him for
our lives and futures, Satan become ticked
off at us.

✴ WHAT OTHER GRIPES DOES SATAN HAVE AGAINST YOU?

Satan is not just upset at you for insulting him and his philosophy,
but you are now actively involved in robbing members from his team
and bringing them to God's.

Romans 6:13
"...and do not go on presenting the members of your body to sin as
instruments(weapons) of unrighteousness; but present yourselves to
God as those alive from the dead and your members as instruments
(weapons) of righteousness to God."

✴ According to this verse, what is your body called? __Weapons__
__For righteousness to God.__

164

IF YOU are LIVING FOR CHRIST...

...you are God's mighty weapon that is fully equipped to rob Satan's kingdom. Satan does not think this is a very good situation. No wonder the Bible says:

I Peter 5:8
"Be of sober spirit, be on the alert. Your adversary, the devil, prowls about like a roaring lion, seeking someone to devour."

SO YOU NEED TO GET READY...

...since we are involved in a continual warfare against Satan. It might be wise for us to learn his methods of attack and how to best defend ourselves against him and his methods.

CATCH THIS THOUGHT:

Attacks from Satan can come directly from him, through the world's thought system, or from the flesh (our own sin nature which so quickly agrees with the ways of Satan).

A MAJORITY OF STUDENTS...

...are tempted most often in the area of the flesh. The flesh stems from our own rebellious sin nature.

WHAT IS THE FLESH?

The flesh is any area of our human nature which is not controlled by God and is therefore prone to sin and rebellion. Satan greatly desires to work through this part of our inner self in an effort to make us rebel against God.

WHAT IS TEMPTATION?

Temptation is the state of being enticed to what is displeasing to God (that which is _wrong_) by a promise of pleasure or gain. Satan and our own selfish lusts are the initiators of temptation.

NOW LET'S GET INTO...

- techniques used by our rebellious nature in order to cause us to sin
- the final results of that sin
- some steps to take that will help us to defend ourselves against the attacks

I. *OUR REBELLIOUS NATURE HAS TECHNIQUES TO LEAD US INTO SIN*

James 1:14-16
"But each one is tempted when he is carried away and enticed by his own lust. Then when lust has conceived, it gives birth to sin; and when sin is accomplished, it brings forth death. Do not be deceived, my beloved brethren."

Verse 14 is very important because it tells of the culprit which entices us to sin and also of the subtle devices it uses in an effort to mess up our lives. The culprit:

"OUR OWN LUSTS!"

 What is lust? _____

Desires are basic components of each human life. We have been created with deep desires for God. When man rebelled against God, his attitudes became those which did not want to please God, and these intensified with the intent to do evil. Man's heart, apart from God's control, will always want to do the opposite of God's will.

GOD'S WILL

MY WILL

James 1:14
"But each one is tempted when he is carried away and enticed by his own lust."

This verse reveals the first technique that our own sin nature uses against us to encourage us to fall into sin.

STAGE #1: THE "CARRIED-AWAY" OR "CURIOSITY" STAGE

This is the subtle trick of our own lust to get us curious about sin. The plan of our own lust is to convince us to leave the security of doing right. It wants to get us out into the "danger zone" where sin can really have its effect on us. Since sin is so readily available to us, it is often easy for curiosity to lead us into this "danger zone." Some examples of how curiosity can manipulate us:

Here is PAT PORNO.
His problem is dirty books and magazines. He knows where the magazine racks are at the store, and he tells himself, "I'm not going to look at all those books, but I would like to know if there is anything new on the market, to see how bad these kinds of magazines really are!"

LOOK OUT PAT PORNO!
You have just been manipulated by your own lust! Curiosity is using you!

LUST 4x4 Porn

RAW FILTH LS

SEX

SINSATIONAL NEW MAGS!!!

Meet **HELEN HEAVY.**

She is overweight because she overeats, not because she ~~one~~ "has a gland problem." Helen is on a diet. Every day on her way home from school she passes the local ice cream store. She hears that the store is offering ten new flavors. "Knowing" she won't eat any ice cream, she wanders into the store just to find out what new flavors might be there.

LOOK OUT HELEN HEAVY!

<u>*You will be manipulated by your own lusts! That curiosity will get you into trouble!*</u>

Meet **DAN DRINKER.**

Dan is a student with a drinking problem. He has quit drinking because it is easy for him to get drunk, but he's curious to find out what's going on over at the drinking party this Friday night. He's not going to drink, he tells himself, but he just wants to see what's happening at the party.

LOOK OUT DAN DRINKER!

<u>*You have just been manipulated by your own lusts, and are about to be totally deceived!*</u>

Here is **MARY MATERIALISM.**

She has a deep desire for nice clothes--lots and lots of nice clothes! She does not need a new outfit, but there's a big sale at the local department store. She tells herself she won't buy anything... She just wants to see what kind of bargains they have so maybe she can tell her mother or her friends about the neat things on sale!

LOOK OUT MARY MATERIALISM

<u>*You have just been sucked in and manipulated by your lusts!*</u>

STAGE #2: THE "ENTICEMENT" STAGE

Once led through the "curiosity stage," our lusts will cause us to enter the "enticement" stage of temptation.

✳ What is the enticement stage?

(This is when the pleasure of sin is offered as something so wonderful and so satisfying, that a person will want to pursue it with all of his efforts. Our lust offers us the "big promise" of delight and pleasure.)

Fishing offers an excellent example of enticement. One will drop a line into the water allowing the fish to see the bait, but not the vicious hooks beneath the bait. Once a fish swallows the bait, it's too late; the fish is hooked. Being enticed to sin is much like this. Beneath many sinful pleasures are the hooks of pain and an awful end.

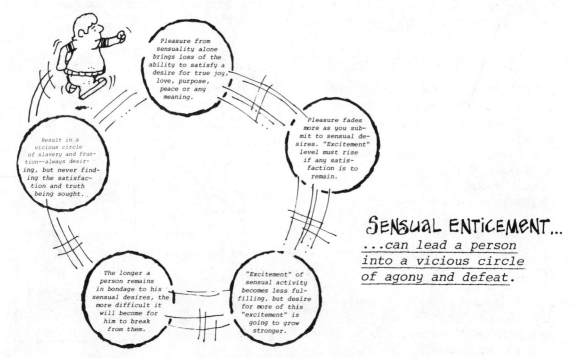

Pleasure from sensuality alone brings loss of the ability to satisfy a desire for true joy, love, purpose, peace or any meaning.

Pleasure fades more as you submit to sensual desires. "Excitement" level must rise if any satisfaction is to remain.

"Excitement" of sensual activity becomes less fulfilling, but desire for more of this "excitement" is going to grow stronger.

The longer a person remains in bondage to his sensual desires, the more difficult it will become for him to break from them.

Result in a vicious circle of slavery and frustration--always desiring, but never finding the satisfaction and truth being sought.

SENSUAL ENTICEMENT...

...can lead a person into a vicious circle of agony and defeat.

STAGE #3: THE "CONCEPTION" STAGE

Up to this point, your lust has been
diligently at work. It began by using
your natural curiosity to lure you into
a situation where you were very vulnerable
to sin. Then lust told you a lie--that the
pleasure at hand is absolutely important and that you _need_ to have it.
If you've come along this far, _listening to your lust_, you are headed
directly into the next deadly step, the "conception" stage.

James 1:15
"Then when lust has conceived, it gives birth to sin; and when sin is
accomplished, it brings forth death."

LET'S DEFINE THE CONCEPTION STAGE:

When a man's weak will yields to lust and then follows it, the conception
stage has begun. Man has allowed lust to take over his will.

STAGE #4: THE "BIRTH-OF-SIN" STAGE

Sin is never passive. Both Satan and our sin natures entice us to be
active concerning our involvement in sin. They would like to see us
being forced to move down the wrong road. Sin may start within our
minds, but remember that our minds are active.

Matthew 5:27-28

*"You have heard that it was said, 'You shall not commit adultery';
but I say to you, that everyone who looks at a woman to lust for her
has committed adultery with her in his heart."*

<u>Sin may also be outgoing and visible, such as drinking,
misuse of sex, gossiping, laziness, etc.</u>

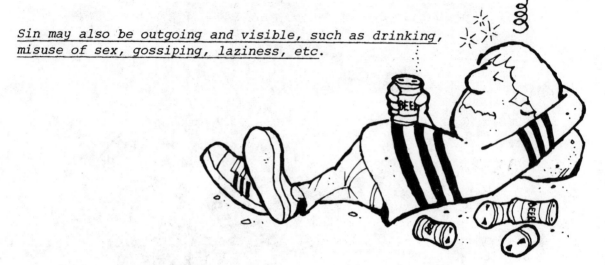

STAGE #5: THE "SIN-MATURING" STAGE

*One would think that Satan and our lust had gotten everything they
wanted from us by now, but that is not the case. They desire for sin
to come to full fruition at this stage. Your own lust's design is
for you to form a bad habit. A person can sin and seemingly get
away with it, but what actually happens is that he will form a pattern
that will do great harm to his life.*

<u>The pattern goes like this:</u>

THOUGHTS *lead to* ACTION!!!

ACTION *leads to* HABIT!!!

HABIT *leads to* MORE ACTION!!!

MORE ACTION *leads to* DISASTER!!!

STAGE #6: THE "MORAL LAW" STAGE

*Once sin forms into a habit, a certain moral law goes into effect.
This is the moral law of death.*

James 1:15

*"Then when lust has conceived, it gives birth to sin; and when sin is
accomplished <u>it brings forth death.</u>"*

LET'S DEFINE DEATH

*In this case, to the Christian, death does
not mean external judgment or even necessarily physical death(although sin does
lead ultimately to physical death). It means
<u>wrong</u> existence--existing in a way that God
never intended.*

HERE ARE SOME EXAMPLES OF WRONG EXISTENCE WHICH GOD ORIGINALLY INTENDED THAT WE NOT HAVE TO HAVE:

1. guilt--God doesn't want this feeling to dominate our lives
2. slavery--being a slave to a pattern of habits in life
3. low self worth--the "I'm-nothing-and-never-will-be" syndrome
4. constant worry--mentally dwelling on the worst that might be
5. broken relationships--living in and with the results of these
6. wasting time

DON'T BE FAKED OUT!

Don't be faked out by sin!
It always leads to wrong existence.
There never has been and never will be
a person who can break this law and
get away with it.

II. *WHAT DO WE DO WHEN TEMPTATION STRIKES?*

A. Recognize the plan of attack.

I Peter 5:8
"Be of sober spirit, be on the alert. Your adversary, the devil, prowls about like a roaring lion, seeking someone to devour."

* What is our responsibility as we face Satan's actions? _____

_____

Jeremiah 17:9
"The heart is more deceitful than all else,
And is desperately sick;
Who can understand it?"

171

IT'S BETTER NOT TO GET IN!

When temptation hits you, ask yourself, "What stage of temptation am I in--the curiosity stage, enticement stage, or what?" It is much easier to flee temptation in the early stages than if you're waist deep in sin. Half the battle is won if you are aware of the devices and the techniques of temptation...

B. Recognize that you are incapable of facing a temptation and of conquering it successfully in your own strength. You must know that the key to victory is in the power of the Holy Spirit working through you.

Galatians 5:16
"But I say, walk by the Spirit, and you will not carry out the desire of the flesh."

GIVE THIS A TRY!

If you are encountering temptation, pray a prayer similar to this:

"Lord, my sin nature is acting up. I know that there is nothing good in me. I can't get out of this situation on my own, in my own strength. Help me flee by filling me with your Holy Spirit."

C. When facing temptation that is caused by youthful lust, FLEE the situation--get out of there as fast as you can!

II Timothy 2:22
"Now flee from youthful lusts, and pursue righteousness, faith, love, love, and peace, with those who call on the Lord from a pure heart."

✳ What does it mean to flee? _____

_____

D. Realize that a key to conquering temptation is to be around friends who really love Christ.

II Timothy 2:22
"Now flee from youthful lusts, and _pursue righteousness, faith,_
love, and peace, with those who call on the Lord from a pure heart."

* What attribute should we be striving for as we spend time with our
friends? _____

* How do you think Christian friends can help you face temptation? _____

_____

James 5:16
"Therefore, confess your sins to one another, and pray for one another,
so that you may be healed. The effective prayer of a righteous man
can accomplish much."

E. _Recognize the positive results of being obedient to God rather_
than disobedient.

James 1:17
"Every good thing bestowed and every perfect gift is from above, coming
down from the Father of lights, with whom there is no variation, or
shifting shadow."

* Does it seem logical that God would give bad gifts to those who obey
Him? _____

* What are the positive results of obeying God? _____

_____

* What are the consequences of disobeying God? _____

_____

LET IT HAPPEN!

Properly handling temptation and
staying clear from the sway of sin is
a most important key to maintaining
happiness. Sin, which flows from
disobedience, causes the Christian
such heartache. Obedience to God
and victory over temptation causes
the heart to soar with the joy and
exhilaration of God's strength.

IN CONCLUSION:

1. Become familiar with the stages of temptation.
2. Learn what to do when temptation strikes.
3. Fill your mind with God's Word, which will bring confidence for facing temptation.

I Corinthians 10:31
"Whether, then, you eat or drink or whatever you do, do all to the glory of God."

TODAY MORE THAN EVER BEFORE STUDENTS ARE ASKING
THE QUESTIONS, — — "IS CHRISTIANITY PRACTICAL?"
"WHAT WILL IT DO FOR ME?"

THE FOLLOWING SERIES OF MANUALS DEAL WITH GOD'S
ANSWERS TO STUDENTS' NEEDS IN A PRACTICAL WAY.

DISCUSSION MANUAL for STUDENT DISCIPLESHIP

Written by Dawson McAllister and Dan Webster

CHAPTER TITLE

DESCRIPTION

The Importance of Your New Life • • •   This chapter deals with our newly established relationship with God through Jesus.

The Importance of God's Love • • • •   Learning to deal with sin on a daily
and Forgiveness   basis and understanding the completeness of God's forgiveness is discussed in this section.

The Importance of Your Trials • • • •   Understanding trials, why we have them, and how God uses them are the topics in this chapter.

The Importance of The Word • • • •   This important section reaffirms the importance and reliability of God's Word in the believers life.

The Importance of Your Quiet Time • •   Spending time daily in God's Word is essential to spiritual growth. Practical "how to's" are given in this chapter.

The Importance of Your Prayer • • •   A scriptural and motivational basis for prayer is discussed in this chapter.

The Importance of the Spirit- • • •   The key to this section is its simplicity
Filled Life   in answering the questions--Who is the Holy Spirit? Why did He come? What is His role?

The Importance of Walking in • • • •   How to allow God Himself to live His life
the Spirit   through us on a daily basis is discussed in this section.

The Importance of Your Fellowship • •   This chapter explains the importance of the Christian student spending time with other Christians.

The Importance of Sharing Your • • •   The goal of this chapter is to introduce
Faith   students to the joy and excitement of introducing others to Jesus Christ and motivate them in a positive way to witness.

DISCUSSION MANUAL for STUDENT DISCIPLESHIP

Written by Dawson McAllister and John Miller

Volume 2

CHAPTER TITLE

DESCRIPTION

The Importance of Obedience • • • • • • This chapter deals with our responsibility to God in regard to our living a successful Christian life.

Learning to Obey God • • • • • • • • • This continues the theme of chapter 1, with specific application concerning our being obedient.

Worship • • • • • • • • • • • • • • • • The importance of worship as a lifestyle is discussed here.

The Christian and the
Lordship of Christ • • • • • • • • • • This chapter is the very essence of the Christian life. Learning to let Christ be Lord is the key to a successful lifestyle.

The Christian Life and
Endurance • • • • • • • • • • • • • • Many Christians start out in a blaze of glory but end in disaster. This chapter deals with the Christian and endurance.

The Responsibility of Love • • • • • • Learning to love one another in Christ is dealt with in this chapter.

Our Responsibility Toward
Other Christians • • • • • • • • • • The importance of our relationships with other Christians is discussed here.

How to Start Your Own
Ministry • • • • • • • • • • • • • • Jesus taught us not to only hear His words. This chapter gives helpful and creative ways of starting your own ministry.

CHaPTeR TiTLe

DeSCriPTioN

The Importance of Understanding
The Bible, A Counselling Book

The value and wisdom the Bible can shed
on everyday life is discussed here.

The Importance of Knowing
God's Will

Whom should I marry? What school should
I attend? What vocation should I pursue?
are questions this chapter will help
answer.

The Importance of a Balanced
Self-Image

This chapter shares how God sees us and
how to form a proper self-image.

The Importance of Dealing
with Loneliness

One of the biggest problems the American
faces is loneliness. This chapter gives
answers on how to deal with this problem.

The Importance of Understanding
Parents

Few relationships affect our lives as do
our relationship with our parents. The
problems and solutions are shared in
this chapter.

The Importance of Understanding
Sex

This section deals with the rationale of
why God's saying what He does about sex.

The Importance of Understanding
Dating

This chapter gives insight into questions
such as--What are the problems in dating?
What should I look for in a date? Does
God have a plan for my date life?

The Importance of Understanding
Love

This work deals with some of the differen
between love and infatuation.

The Importance of Clearing The
Mind

The importance of thinking pure and Godly
thoughts are discussed in this chapter.

The Importance of Dealing With
Temptation

Being tempted and knowing who tempts us is
not always easy to recognize. This
chapter gives practical insights in the
whole area of temptation.

The New TEACHER'S GUIDE

Makes the Discussion Manual

Easy and Complete to Teach!

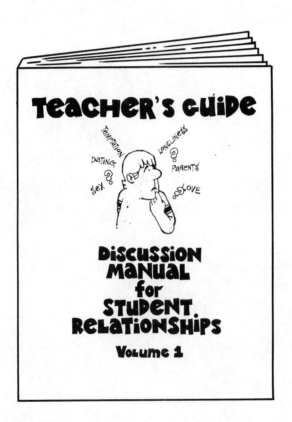

You Get:
- 26 Lessons in Outline Form
- Over 30 Projects
- Additional Bible References
- Hundreds of Questions
- Many Illustrations and Applications
- Lesson Aim and Goals
- Plus, Built-in Teacher Training Tips

Get this comprehensive TEACHER'S GUIDE today!

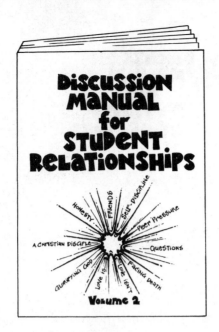

Discussion Manual for Student Relationships

Honesty · Friends · Self-Discipline · Peer Pressure · A Christian Disciple · Questions · Glorifying God · Love Is... · Love Isn't · Facing Death

Volume 2

Chapter Title

Description

How to Glorify God . . . .
Glorifying God and how to do it can be difficult to understand and teach. This simple chapter gets to the heart of glorifying God.

Discipleship . . . .
This chapter shares the answers to the questions, What does it mean to be a disciple of Jesus? Where do I begin?

Love . . . .
Using I Corinthians 13 as its guide this chapter clearly defines what true love is.

What Love Is Not . . . .
Again using the love chapter as its basis this chapter explains what love is not.

Questions on Dating . . . .
The author of the manual Dawson McAllister, answers questions high school students across the country are asking on dating.

Peer Group Pressure . . . .
One of the strongest influences in our lives is the thoughts and actions of our peers towards us. In this discussion we learn how to deal with this pressure.

Making Friends . . . .
This chapter stresses the importance of learning how to make friends and the type of friends God desires for us to have.

Honesty . . . .
Honesty is often rejected in a world where personal gain is more important than trustworthiness. Here we investigate the results of being dishonest and the benefits of honesty.

This book is a must for the youth library.

CHAPTER TITLE

DESCRIPTION

How To Deal With Cliques • • • • This chapter deals with the ever common problem of cliques in a youth group, what God has to say about cliques and how to deal with bitterness toward the elite.

What To Do When Your Boyfriend Or Girlfriend "Drops You" • • • • Being rejected by someone we date and care about is very difficult to handle. This chapter relates to us dealing with broken hearts.

God's View Of The Misuse Of Drugs And Alcohol • • • • • • • This in depth discussion shares why God is absolutely against the misuse of drugs & alcohol. This work gives a positive answer to the problem -- the person of Jesus Christ.

How To Break Bad Habits • • • • Recognizing bad habits and learning how to break them is the topic of this chapter. Deep and practical truths are explained to the Christian on how to deal with sin.

How To Develop New Healthy Habits • This important section, in a very practical way helps explain how to begin to form new and healthy habits.

How To Live In A Broken Home • • • Living in a broken home and allowing God's love to mend some of the hurts isn't easy. This chapter gives some insights into this area.

How To Deal With Guilt • • • • Every student at one time or another faces the emotional pressure of guilt. This sections simply shares how God deals with guilt. This chapter is a must for any youth worker who does counseling.

The Christian Student And Rock Music • • • • • • • • The authors give insight into the advantages and disadvantages of listening to rock music and some creative alternatives.

Discipling Your Time • • • • • Time is one of the most important commodities we have. This chapter deals with how to make the most of our time.

How to Face Death • • • • • • One thing we will all experience is death. This chapter answers the questions--What is death? Why is there death? Where does one go when he/she dies?